PLAY POKER
LIKE A
PIGEON

PLAY POKER LIKE A PIGEON

AND TAKE THE MONEY HOME

Anonymous

LYLE
STUART

Kensington Publishing Corp.
www.kensingtonbooks.com

LYLE STUART BOOKS are published by

Kensington Publishing Corp.
850 Third Avenue
New York, NY 10022

All Kensington titles, imprints, and distributed lines are available at special quantity discounts for bulk purchases for sales promotions, premiums, fund-raising, educational, or institutional use. Special book excerpts or customized printings can also be created to fit specific needs. For details, write or phone the office of the Kensington special sales manager: Kensington Publishing Corp., 850 Third Avenue, New York, NY 10022, attn: Special Sales Department, phone 1-800-221-2647.

Lyle Stuart is a trademark of Kensington Publishing Corp.

First printing: April 2007

10 9 8 7 6 5 4 3 2 1

Printed in the United States of America

ISBN-13: 978-0-8184-0718-5
ISBN-10: 0-8184-0718-2

Contents

PLAY POKER
LIKE A
PIGEON

1

Imagine That It's You . . .

Moving at a hesitant gait through the casino at Las Vegas's Bellagio, approaching the entry to the poker room. You blink in the glare. Your gaze darts from side to side like that of a frightened deer. You're hatless, don't wear sunglasses, and the skin around your eyes is fish-belly white. The brand-new size XXL I Love Las Vegas T-shirt that you're wearing still shows its packaging creases. Your shirttail's out, and flaps loosely over plaid Bermuda shorts. You also wear calf-high white athletic socks and white Pro Walkers. Your knees are freshly sunburned.

You enter the poker lounge, and look past rows of long, low oblong tables toward the back corner, where a short flight of stairs leads up to the Bellagio's legendary high players' room. That's high as in high—as in Doyle Brunson, Phil Hellmuth, Howard Lederer/ Annie Duke/Jennifer Harman–type high, the special room up there where the biggest games in the world go on every day. Your jaw is slack in awe.

It takes effort, but you walk to the back of the room and place one foot on the bottom step. At the last moment you lose your nerve; you dare not enter the high rollers' lair. Instead you turn around and approach the poker desk and inquire in a quaking voice about joining a game. You'd like to play Texas Hold 'Em, preferably ten- and twenty-dollar limit, fifteen- and thirty-dollar limit if the less expensive game isn't available. Though two- and three-thousand-dollar wins or losses are common in each of the games you've mentioned, they're considered cheap in comparison to what's going on at the top of those steps you're afraid to climb.

There's a hip young woman behind the desk, dressed in slacks and a blazer with the Bellagio logo on the pocket. She looks you over and at the same time signals a floor man with a slight movement of her head. Down the line a house shill gets a tap on the shoulder and has to give up his seat; for live ones like you, the games are never full. The casino hostess smiles broadly and tells you you're in luck; there's an opening in the fifteen-and-thirty game.

You pull out enough wadded-up, oft-circulated twenty-dollar bills to total five hundred bucks. As you're counting out your cookie-jar money, a man strolls up and buys a thousand dollars' worth of chips, showing you a sneering glance as he slides a stack of crisp new hundreds across the counter. You grin sheepishly and continue to count your twenty-dollar bills, smoothing each one out as you form a ratty-looking stack of money. The casino employee watches with a smile of patience that looks a bit strained. When you're finished she counts the twenties, stuffs your money away into a cash drawer, grabs a rack of five-dollar chips, and leads you to your seat in the fifteen-and-thirty. You sit down and ask for a drink. The casino person snaps her fingers, and a cocktail waitress hustles over carrying a tray.

You manage a fearful glance around the table at the competition, all men. Most wear sunglasses and golf hats with World Series of Poker, Golden Nugget, or Bellagio logos, bills down low over their eyes. Some have less-than-original trademarks; there's a Chris (Jesus)

Ferguson look-alike (though Chris Ferguson himself wouldn't be caught dead in a thirty-dollar game) complete with beard and black Zorro hat, and another guy whose iridescent sunglasses have cartoon eyes painted on the lenses. Some players nonchalantly shuffle chips one-handed, or expertly slide single chips from the top of the stack into their palms, one after another, with flicks of their thumbs. All show you deadpan looks.

You swallow hard, order a beer, and pull your own chips out of the rack to stack them. Once you've created a semi-orderly fortress of five-dollar chips, you accidentally bump the pile with your elbow and your fortress collapses into a jumbled mess. You fumble your chips into patternless stacks, your cheeks red with embarrassment.

So, who's the sucker here?

If you know what you're doing, *they* are. That's right, the expert chip shufflers and sunglasses-wearing guys.

Really.

Read on.

2

We Gotta Have Purpose Here

Just as you should've already gathered from the title, the purpose of this book is to help the reader become a really good poker player, but at the same time create the illusion that he or she is a card-playing Dumbo who will bring an easily won infusion of cash into a game. As you read on you're going to think, Christ, this guy is beating his point to death. We *get it* already; he wants us to fool people into thinking that we're pigeons when really we're not. Well, maybe *you* get it, but trust me, not everyone does.

It's a hard fact of life that many businesses prosper by taking money from people who *don't* get it, and that's true no matter if you're hustling poker for profit, pushing stocks down on Wall Street, or selling encyclopedias door to door. Granted there are varying degrees of don't-get-it-ness, all the way from those who are totally clueless about everything to people who are really smart about some things but really dumb about others. And then there are those who are brilliant about most things, and really smart about lots of things that they aren't totally brilliant about, but still don't get certain aspects of things that they otherwise have figured out to a T. Just about everyone fails to get *something*— even you, and especially me. Poker is a game that can make the world's smartest people seem as dumb as fence posts.

For example, some will read this book thinking that it's a how-to manual on the form of poker called Texas Hold 'Em. It's true that Hold 'Em is the only game we're going to discuss at length, but that's because Hold 'Em is the only poker game worth talking about since television has made the nation Texas Hold 'Em crazy. Everybody's playing it, and in today's climate, you'd best learn Texas Hold 'Em or give up poker altogether. So those who think that this is an instruction book on Hold 'Em will be right— up to a point—but they'll be missing the overall picture. Once again: If you become good at disguising your skill level, you will keep the other players off balance no matter whether you're playing Hold 'Em, deuce-to-seven low ball, Razz, Omaha, or any other form of poker, and it's my goal to hammer this point home if it kills both you and me.

Also, some readers will be disappointed because this book deals almost exclusively with *limit* Texas Hold 'Em rather than the sky-high, shove-it-all-in showdowns featured in the World Series of Poker, the International Poker Superstars, the Poker Stars' Invitational, the Bet Your Butt Off Poker Whizzes' Reunion, the Giggle-When-You've-Got-Something Has-Been Celebrities' Poker Showdown, the Ass on the Line Shootout, the Gutsy Players' Open, and whatever other made-for-television fiascos are showing right now. There are a couple of reasons for restricting most of this book's discussions to limit poker, the main one being that, no matter what you hear on ESPN, the most skillful player in limit poker will come out ahead in the long run 100 percent of the time, while in no-limit poker an inferior player can take the better player's entire bankroll in one poorly played, dumb-lucky hand. I make this statement knowing full well that some poker players, even some who are supposed to know what they're talking about, will argue that no-limit poker is the only Real Players' Game. Well, those poker players are dead wrong, and not only that: televised no-limit poker completely distorts the most effective methods of playing even *that* game, for a myriad of reasons. Here are just a few.

First of all, television shows only freeze-out tournaments that require a completely different strategy than cash-on-the-barrelhead games, the real player's lifeblood. TV tourneys exist at the whim of producers who believe—correctly, by the way—that the higher the stakes, the larger the audience that will tune in. But know this: Televised tournament players' losses are limited to their original buy-ins (not to mention that in certain of these tourneys, the television producers have furnished the big-name players' buy-ins, so the players have *nothing* at risk). When "Action" Dan Harrington shoves four hundred thousand chips into the pot, he's really not shoving in anything but stamped and decorated pieces of clay, and the four hundred thousand that the announcer screams about is mere Monopoly money. Each player bought into the tournament with the same amount—in the World Series Main Event it's ten thousand dollars, and there are other competitions in the annual shootout at the Rio and Horseshoe with buy-ins as low as a thousand bucks—and that figure is all that a player can lose (not to mention that more than half of the Main Event participants have won their seats in satellite online tournaments with buy-ins as low as twenty-five dollars).

Furthermore, from a learning standpoint, the quality of the play on television ranges from average to poor to terrible, even though the players involved are often some of the finest in the world. There. I've said it, and I'm never taking it back. This is particularly true at a tournament's final table, where the structure of the game makes really skillful play impossible. Oddly enough the sloppy play is not the fault of the participants but primarily of television producers and host casinos who insist that the tournament cannot go on beyond the scheduled time frame. The best way to ensure that the tournament ends in time for the Partypoker.com commercial is to raise the amount of the blinds (the two forced bets that open each hand before the cards are dealt) as player elimination shrinks the field. At the World Series of Poker's final table, the blinds generally start at 30,000 and 60,000 chips, and build from there until the final heads-up twosome is putting up 100,000 and 200,000 per hand, and if players don't play in pots that they wouldn't dream of playing in a cash game, their forced blinds will eventually take all of their chips away and they'll lose by default. Watching two dead-serious, sunglasses-wearing guys shove mountains of chips into the pot as the tournament reaches its climax makes for good theater, but in truth the players who reach the World Series final table might just as well put all of their chips in the center and cut high card to determine the champion. As the Monster Bucks grow nearer, skillful play pretty much goes out the window.

But the main reason that we're going to deal almost exclusively with limit poker is that you're trying to convince people that you don't know what you're doing. You can look stupid, knock your chips over with your elbow, and demonstrate your lack of cool by calling two queens a "pair of ladies" or two aces a "couple of bullets" until the cows come home, but the second you sidle up to the big no-limit tables, then walk away a winner, your pigeon's badge will be tarnished beyond repair. You can make a nice living in the fifteen-and-thirty and thirty-and-sixty games without getting your picture on television, and if you buy into this book's philosophy, that's exactly what you'll try to do.

And by the way, I'm not the only one who feels that in order to guarantee profit you should stick to the limit games. The famous Big Game played upstairs at the Bellagio every day is a limit game—granted, the limits are astronomical, $4,000 and $8,000 most days—and what is probably the biggest poker game ever played (actually a series of head-up games at the Bellagio, pitting a deep-pocketed Dallas banker named Andy Beal against a tag team gang of marquee pros with Doyle Brunson as their coach and game organizer) was in fact limit poker—$30,000 and $60,000 at some points, but limit poker nonetheless. So while the high-dollar pros play in no-limit tournaments for the benefit of the TV audience, when their money is on the line in cash competitions, even they revert to a limit game.

And for a final argument in favor of limit poker, just look at casino games such as craps and blackjack. Everybody knows that the odds are against them when they square off against the house, yet for some reason thousands upon thousands play the sucker games anyway. If you're considered a high-roller (known among casino personnel as a Whale, in honor of a big, blubbery, not overly bright sea creature), you can get free plane rides, plush hotel rooms on the cuff, the finest food available, free tickets to the lushest of shows, sex if you want, or just about anything your heart desires, as long as you'll play.

At the Whale's request the casino stakes can go higher than the house limits, but *under no circumstances* will the Whale be allowed to play *without* a limit, because the house knows that a single huge wager, if won, can knock their percentages out of the tub. So sticking to limit poker works the same way as the system that has built all those luxury hotels: Play with the percentages in your favor, restrict the maximum bets, and through continued rock-solid play, let the passage of time increase your bankroll.

For the benefit of those readers who must have it come hell or high water, however, I've included a chapter at the end of this book dealing with no-limit poker and tournament strategy. Let me

say right here and now, though, that I don't recommend tournaments—or any other form of no-limit poker for that matter—
for us Pigeons Who Would Be Winners. But as I said at the outset
of this chapter, there are people around who never seem to get
it. Sad but true.

3

Laying It Out in Computerese

I'm from the Dark Age Before Computers, and am new at this browsing-through-websites business, but it seems that nearly every site I visit has, on its homepage, a place for you to click on marked "Frequently Asked Questions." I suspect that this section could be better titled "Dumb Questions That You Morons Are Probably Going to Ask," and on visiting these sites I generally disdain from clicking on Frequently Asked Questions and show my irritation at being lumped in with Those Too Dumb to Think Up Anything Original by e-mailing my stupid questions to the website staff anyway.

But, you know, when in Rome . . . Since the bulk of my audience is from a different time and therefore predominantly computer hip, I now give you my own list of Frequently Asked Questions. Feel free to show your irritation by ignoring my list and e-mailing your questions to me at pigeon3450@yahoo.com. I'll answer within forty-eight hours or my name ain't . . . oh, never mind.

Wait, I'm getting ahead of myself. Since we're using the website model in this chapter, even before the list of Frequently Asked Questions there should be a disclaimer, a section where the site gives its terms and you must click on ACCEPT or DECLINE, and where, should you decline, you are to be automatically banished from the website. So in line with that protocol, please check out the following disclaimer:

DO NOT, UNDER ANY CIRCUMSTANCES, FOLLOW THE TEACHINGS OF THIS BOOK IF . . .

(a) You want to be a television star and give interviews to people like Norman Chad, and make statements like "I've always been a superior player but this is my chance to be known in the poker world" or "It's not the money—gotta have that bracelet" while seated at a poker table with gigantic piles of chips in front of you. I advocate *not* being known. If you gotta be known, go elsewhere.

(b) You want to be on a first-name basis with pit bosses, poker room managers, or the before-mentioned Doyle, Phil, Howard, Annie, Jennifer, and the gang. Not that these folks aren't lovely people and entertaining to be around (which they are with a few exceptions), but you just don't want others to lump you in with a gang of pros. You're the pigeon. Act like one.

(c) You have a tendency to make sneering remarks to other players who've just drawn out to beat you, such as, "You played *king, four?*" or, "If we sit here long enough I'm gonna own you," thus establishing yourself as a poker expert-slash-asshole, and also causing you to fit right in at the Bellagio, Mirage, and various other points along the Las Vegas strip and downtown. You want to be thought of as a player who'll jump into a pot with K4, or any other two-card combination for that matter. Remember, you're too dumb to "own" anyone, and have just barely enough sense to find your way to the poker table. As far as you know, K4 is just as good as AA, 92, or any other hand.

Accept? Decline? If you decline, close this book immediately and put it away. Otherwise go on to the meat of the book's topic, which is as follows:

DO READ THIS BOOK IF YOU WANT TO AVOID THE LIMELIGHT, YET BE A CONSISTENT WINNER AT THE POKER TABLE.

That's it. That's the one and only reason to buy this book. This is no book for beginners; it's an instruction manual for already fairly competent players who want to move to the next level while not letting other players realize what they're up against. There's no shortage of other material out, written by seemingly everyone who's ever won a hand of poker on television, so if (a), (b), or (c) above better suits your goals, put this book down, right now, and move on to one of those.

Still with me? If you are, now for—ta-*taaa*—the Poker Pigeon's List of Frequently Asked Questions. Feel free to click on any or all of the following:

Q. So who the hell are you?

A. Good question. The answer, though, is "none of your business," for reasons that should be obvious. If the writer of a book wants to remain anonymous (unless he's writing a hatchet job/novel whose main character is a thinly disguised version of a recent U.S. president, and really doesn't want to remain anonymous but actually wants his identity later revealed to a breathless nation), then for all you know he might be an escapee from a mental institution, a fugitive from justice, or the guy down the block who doesn't know his ass from his elbow about poker but wants to write a book about it. Or there's a chance that he's actually an expert professional poker player who doesn't want his cover blown. If I say I'm the Pro in Disguise, then you might or might not believe me, so I think I'll just let you make up your own mind which description fits me. You can take my advice seriously and try it out in real play or, since my teachings will often be the direct opposite of what you'll hear elsewhere, you can read this book strictly for belly laughs over how dumb the author is. Either way this book will entertain you, and if you follow the advice given here you just might become a better poker player. Like all things financial, the proof is in the bottom line.

Q. Well, then, how many world series bracelets you got? Can't write no book about poker without a bunch of bracelets, homes.

A. Nice try. But if I have ever won any World Series events and I answer that question truthfully, then you could go to the WSOP website, look up all the bracelet winners since 1970, and figure out who I am by process of elimination. I haven't played in a World Series event in a number of years—I'll tell you that much (though I've been to Las Vegas and played in side games nearly every year while the WSOP was going on)—and I'll also say that I'm haunted more by two titles that I *didn't* capture than by any I might've won.

More than two decades ago, during the first of Stu Ungar's three World Series wins, he knocked me out of the tournament just prior to going on to the final table. In the pivotal hand I held AA to Stuey's QJ. He called my substantial raise before the flop, which turned out to be A,Q,4. I made a small initial bet, trying to trap him with my set of aces, and to my shock Ungar moved all in, right then and there. I've never been sure whether he was stone-cold bluffing or he thought his pair of queens were the best hand, but he showed his trademark little-kid smirk as all of his chips went to the center of the table. At the time I had the nuts (pokerese for the best possible hand in relation to the cards on the board), so of course I called. Actually Stu had a few more chips than I, so if he'd lost the hand he wouldn't have been eliminated, though the winner of the hand would assume a commanding chip lead. The stage was set. The dealer prepared to deliver the final two cards to Stuey and me, along with a packed house and a breathless nation. You could cut the tension with a saw.

I turned my cards faceup.

Ungar's expression sagged in despair. He showed his QJ and sadly watched the ceiling.

So there I sat, my cards visible to the world, waiting for the dealer to produce two more off the deck, then to send Ungar packing. In minutes I'd be ready for my parade to the center of the poker universe.

But something funny happened on my way to international stardom. The turn and the river cards were both spades, as were the ace and queen that had come on the flop, so the hand ended up with four spades on the board. The jack in Stuey's hand was the jack of spades, and the aces in my hand were both red, so he'd made a flush while I was left with my pitiful set of aces. The odds against Ungar winning that pot, both before, and especially after, the flop, were astronomical, but nonetheless he did. Let it suffice to say that the hand has haunted me for more than twenty-five years. (Did I mention that people drawing out on me just drives me up a tree? Well, it does, and learning to control my temper in those situations is the hardest thing I've ever done in poker. Today I'd give Stuey a warm handshake and congratulate the guy. Back then, after I'd picked myself up off the floor, I think I sneered and shot him the finger. For all the good it did. You're never going to be a quality player until you learn to control your temper. Think golf. The difference in the physical effort required between poker and golf is considerable, but the proper mental state for playing each is exactly the same.)

Less than a year after I experienced what I've come to call the Stu Ungar Miracle, I enjoyed the next milestone in my career, which in my mind is known as the Welcome Back Kotter Killing. Actor/comedian Gabe Kaplan is a fine player, and to his credit he's still around a quarter century later and playing strong, but the licking he gave me on his way to winning Amarillo Slim's Super Bowl of Poker at the Sahara Tahoe was one for the record books. Kaplan held AK. My pair of sixes was a slight favorite to win the hand, and the 4,4,6 that appeared on the flop put me in the driver's seat with a made full house, and put old Gabe up shit creek in a toilet paper canoe. This was in the unsophisticated era before players' percentage chances of winning the pot flashed on the TV screen, but I think my odds were about 98 percent at that point. I checked. Kaplan made a token bluff, and I called after taking an Oscar-winning period of time to pretend to think about it. The fish was on the line, and I wasn't about to let it wiggle away.

The turn card was, lo and behold, the ace of hearts, a dream card for me, one that gave Kaplan the top pair on the board and practically assured his presence in the pot to the bitter end, even though the only way he could win was to catch one of the two aces remaining in the deck on the river. How much of a favorite was I? Try 21 to 1.

I checked. Kaplan bet. I moved all in, and Kaplan called. I can still see the hesitant look in his eyes and the light reflecting from his beard.

The river card (of course) was the ace of spades, giving him a caught-lightning-in-a-jug hand of aces full, and sending my puny *sixes* full down to defeat. Ready to throw up, my composure gone, beaten once again, I staggered away from the table vowing to never return. And, in fact, after another couple of years battling the pros, I did retire from that arena to go off in search of easier games.

My point? Well, there are actually a *couple* of points I'm trying to make. Stu Ungar was a dyed-in-the-wool professional, and while Kaplan may still list "actor/comedian" as his occupation on his 1040 every year, the guy is in fact a poker pro as well. And in the two hands I've just described, did either of these players make an error? I maintain that Stu Ungar did, though some will disagree. (It's amazing how, when one of the marquee names makes an inexcusable play, someone—usually the TV announcer—comes to the star's defense by saying that his strategy is so advanced that us mortals just don't understand.) But Kaplan played his hand perfectly, and I'm sure that both Stu and Gabe, if asked, would say that there was nothing lacking in my own play. Texas Hold 'Em, while in the long run is purely a test of skill, is also a game where each individual hand is largely dependent on the luck of the draw, and for reasons I'll go into later, this is true in Hold 'Em more than any other form of poker known to man. Even if you're the best player at the table, your edge is still a small one, and it takes many hours of play for the cream to rise. For you to have any advantage at all there must be players in the game whose skill is less than your own. In Las Vegas there are about fifty pros who equally share the World's Best Player title (though each one of the fifty thinks the title should belong only to him or her), and if ten of those pros played with each other every day for, say, four or five centuries, then they'd all break about even. They don't make their living playing each other; they survive because of the people who drift in and out of the casinos wanting to try their luck against the big dogs. So if you become an expert player, one way to make a living at it is to live in Las Vegas, and if 125-degree summer days are your cup of tea and you crave the limelight, that's exactly what you should do. But if you'd like to exist in more pleasant climes and associate with poker players not as likely to make off with your bankroll, then there are plenty of places to land elsewhere. Which brings us back to the question that pretty well covers the entire theme of this book: Fame or fortune? It's up to you.

My second point is pretty much an extension of the first, though its thrust is a little bit different. I knew Stu Ungar well in the old days, though since he's now dead he'd have a hard time pointing me out to you. As for Gabe Kaplan, at the time he knocked me from Amarillo Slim's tourney, *Welcome Back, Kotter* was in wide syndication and Kaplan was still a major star. Time and memory have dimmed Kaplan's image in the public consciousness, but then he was one of the most famous people in the world. Celebrities by necessity must keep the public at arm's length, so to Kaplan, all the other players in that tournament made up a sea of faces that he didn't recognize. It's better than even money that Gabe remembers the hand I've just described (though it isn't a cinch, since all poker players tend to remember the hands where someone has drawn out on *them* rather than the other way around), but because he's never laid eyes on me since that I'm aware of, the odds are long that he couldn't pick me out of a crowd. And if you follow the teachings of this book, no one should be able to pick you out of a crowd, either. Once again I'm beating this point to death, but there's a method in my madness. You should move unobtrusively from game to game, make your mark in each, then be gone before the others can figure out who the hell that masked man was.

So much for tales of my forays into big-time tournament poker (for now, at least). I've had better luck in the tournaments leading up to the Main Event than I did against Ungar and Kaplan, but I was never again in a position to win the Big One. I guess I wouldn't be human if I didn't occasionally reflect on What Could Have Been, but you know what? If I'd won those two pots I might've been hooked for good on being a Big Time Poker Guy, and might still be chasing that dream today. Funny how things work out. I love my life as it is, and it's better that I lost.

Are the grapes getting a bit sour here?

Well, maybe. Since I never won a Main Event, I'll never know how I would have reacted if Stuey had drawn the four of diamonds and the six of hearts instead of two running (consecutive) spades, or if Kaplan's river card had been the eight of spades instead of one of the two remaining aces in the deck, so all I can do is speculate. I could be a major star, I suppose, but it also could have been me instead of Stu Ungar dead inside that cheap motel with cocaine stuffed up my nose. But why worry about the Road Not Traveled? I've played poker, before then and since then, both in Las Vegas and points around the world, with Doyle Brunson, Puggy Pearson, Bobby Hoff, Slim Preston, Bob Hooks, Bobby Baldwin, Cowboy Wolford, the aforementioned Stu Ungar, and assorted other professionals, and while I won't say I've picked their pockets, I haven't lost anything to those folks. I don't know Hellmuth, Lederer, Ivey, Harman, or any of the younger Las Vegas players because I melted into the background over twenty years ago, so I've never pitted my skills against them and they might be head-and-shoulders better than I. But like most Old Guys Who Think They've Still Got It, I doubt it.

Q. Look, that's all very interesting, but since you won't own up to who you are, what is it that makes me think you know what you're talking about?

A. My record. I quit my last job in 1970. My primary source of income since then has been what I've won playing poker (though

I've done other things, such as run an illegal poker game down in Texas, and—believe it or not—even made a little money from my writing), and I've never missed a car or rent payment and have put four kids through college, and I don't have a single unpaid debt due in the poker world. It's true there is a famous TV star/poker player, a guy you've often seen on ESPN, who owes me six hundred bucks from twenty-five years ago, money that I'll never see. At least I don't *think* I'll ever see it because I've run into this guy twice since he became a television star, and on each occasion I've gotten the same runaround about my six hundred dollars as I did twenty-five years ago. But one never knows. Life is full of surprises. Another guy, this one a World Series Main Event champion, hocked his watch to me two months after he won over $800,000 at Binnion's Horseshoe, and two years after that I sold the watch for twice what he owed me. Another World Series champ, now deceased, once told me that I could sleep with his wife if I'd buy him a half-gallon of whiskey. I passed on the wife but did buy him the whiskey, and later regretted it when the guy drank himself to death. Lots of World Series champs are dead or fallen by the wayside. I'm still here, still in action, and still paying rent, and I haven't heard any yelps of surprise from my landlord when my monthly check arrives.

As for trying to convince you that I know what I'm talking about, well, *no one* has all the answers when it comes to Texas Hold 'Em. I know more about playing the game than do 99.9 percent of the people in the world, at least enough so that you could consider me an authority, though I don't claim to be a better player than any of your television heroes. I do claim to be *equal* in skill to anyone you've seen on ESPN or Fox Sports Network and also claim that my poker life has been much simpler and much more fulfilling since, over twenty years ago, I made the decision to steer clear of those superstars and find myself some easier games. If Ivey and Lederer and Hellmuth and Negreanu and Brunson and Chan and Harman—or whoever—want to bang heads at the Bellagio every day, they should go right ahead; it's their money. But their life ain't for me and never will be again.

Q. Okay, okay, but if you're doing so well as a player, why give your secrets away?

A. Now that's the best question that you've asked so far, and I'm not sure that I can give an answer that's going to satisfy you. As I'm writing this book anonymously, fame is certainly not my motive, and since I'll never make as much money from writing this book as I normally do in just a few months of playing poker, neither is fortune. So let's just say that I've got a bee in my bonnet that won't go away, and putting this all down on paper might be the only way I can get rid of the damned thing as it buzzes around up there. So here we go, and if I get stung in the process, so be it.

A favorite axiom among poker pros is "Never wise up the suckers," even though a vast majority of pros that claim to live by that motto in fact do just the opposite. They sit around the table grousing about the bad beats they've suffered, quoting the exact number of "outs" (winning cards) the sucker had left in the deck before drawing out on the pro, and spouting figures off the top of their heads as to what odds the sucker overcame in winning the hand. Pros who behave in this manner are cutting their own throats. Suckers aren't suckers because they're stupid; they're suckers because no one's ever taught them the right way to play. Any professional who sits around telling the suckers how the previous hand *should* have been played will wake up one day with the suckers all gone, and a gang of poker barracudas on his hands.

Having said that, I will further state that there is one thing which drives me further up a tree than the poker know-it-alls who've inhabited just about every game I've ever played in, and that's the so-called professionals who sound really authoritative while spouting self-assured poker knowledge, *yet still don't know what the hell they are talking about.* Since the guy who's spewing these bits of wisdom is supposed to be a pro, the listener then repeats the wisdom at the next game he plays in, and the first thing you know, total bullshit has spread throughout the poker world and is taken as the gospel. And that's the honest-to-God reason I decided to write this book: to correct some misconceptions that people have, mostly learned from watching poker on television.

Each person's method of doing a thing is the product of that person's experience and, if you're talking about poker, that's true whether you're Doyle Brunson or someone who took up the game ten minutes ago. Brunson's a pro because of what he's learned over the years; the newcomer's a novice because he's yet to learn a single thing. But if he ever accumulates as much experience as Brunson, then his play will be just as good as Brunson's or very close to it. Many of the poker hot shots in Las Vegas and elsewhere don't believe that anyone can be their equal, but Brunson's a whole lot smarter than most of those people. If you ever meet him, ask him. He'll be the first to tell you that what I'm saying in this paragraph is true.

Let's all agree that the only way you can improve your game is to play it and play it often and in as many different environments as possible. Neither this nor any other book will help you get better unless you put its teachings in play and learn from your own results and experiences. This book will help you get a whole lot better a whole lot faster, but if you think you can memorize its contents, then head for the poker room at the Bellagio, forget it. Like a golfer's backswing, you gotta take it low and slow.

Remember: The game of poker is not an exact science, and no book is going to show you how to react in every situation.

You can have every chart in the world showing you the rank of every two-card Hold 'Em hand known to man. You can have Cliff Notes telling you what to do with every hand depending on your position in relation to the button (the button being the little thingy that the dealer moves around to tell him who gets last position in the hand he's about to deal), yet the very next time you play, you will have situations where you should ignore the book and play a few hands depending on who's doing the betting and how many other players have come into the pot before you. Altering your style of play is essential to becoming a superior poker player. This book carries play alteration even a step further, by showing you how to alter your style of play so that the alterations seem to be a hodge-podge of errors on your part. If you walk away from the table a winner, yet with the other players calling you dumb-lucky as they pray for your return, then this book has accomplished its purpose. But if you stroll through a casino card room with players guardedly watching you and saying from the sides of their mouths, "Look out for that guy. He's a *player*," then this book has failed.

So now. Are you ready for Lesson One and the beginning of your descent into pigeondom? It's a fun ride, folks. Hope you tag along.

4

Where to Go and Who to Be

Remember the people who just don't get it, the ones discussed at the beginning of chapter 2? Well, this is the chapter where I'm probably gonna lose those folks. They'll thumb madly through this section in search of real poker instruction and, finding none, go quickly on to the parts of the book dealing with the playing of the game. And even my new disciples, those who are starting to believe that I might know what I'm talking about, will read partway through this chapter and think, *Aw, what's this crap? I wanta know when to raise and when to fold, not all this Andrew Carnegie stuff. I already know how to act, man, I wanta know how to play. I shouldda bought the books by Hellmuth and Brunson and those guys.*

Okay, I'll admit that this chapter is no walk in the park. This is the chapter on finding games where you'll be a heavy favorite to win by following the teachings in this book, and on building the proper pigeon's image. It will get tedious at times, but you've simply got to wade through this material in order to complete the course. Remember logarithms? Think of this chapter as log-arithms.

But, hey—this is also the most important chapter in the book. And you can mark that down for posterity.

It's amazing to me how many people want to look on play-ing poker as a business, yet refuse to treat it as one. A man try-ing for success in the corporate jungle strives from Day One to develop a persona, usually one of take-no-prisoners ruthlessness, as he climbs to the top while leaving a mass of twisted and man-gled bodies in his wake. He oozes intimidation. Don't get in his way or he'll step first *on* you, and then *over* you. Nice guys fin-ish last is Mr. Success's motto. Winning isn't everything, it's the only thing.

On the other hand, a guy trying to make it running an auto repair shop must project an entirely different image. If *he's* going to succeed he must be thought of as friendly, hardworking and honest, a man who looks you straight in the eye and wouldn't lie if his life depended on it. This man wouldn't dream of slouch-ing around in a filthy pair of overalls with tools sticking out of every pocket, a lit cigarette dangling from his lips, leaning his greasy ass against the side of a customer's car. His shop is spot-less. If he tells you that you need motor mounts, you never doubt him.

Playing poker as a business works the same way. If you want to play like a pigeon and take the money home, you must de-velop a persona that will make other players salivate to have you in the game even as you're separating them from their bankrolls. Image is paramount, and if you create the wrong persona you won't succeed no matter how skillful a player you become. You might as well try bailing hay.

Just as in everyday life, you can't begin to form the right image unless you have the lay of the land. So begin with the no-brainer assumption that before you can utilize any of the nifty tricks outlined in this book you have to find a poker game where you can win amounts that will satisfy you and where the competition isn't so stiff that you'll be banging your head against a tree, and go from there. Examine the competition and determine what image will work best for you.

First let's talk about where *not* to play. I've already discussed Las Vegas and its shark-filled waters. Aside from Las Vegas, you must also avoid all "friendly" games where some of "the guys" get together at one of the players' houses once a week, break out the beer, and generally act like a pack of jackasses. This sort of circle jerk will erode your skills through a steady diet of joker-in-the-deck Spit in the Ocean, Low Hole Card Wild, Criss-Cross Draw, etc., etc., etc., with an occasional hand of Hold 'Em thrown in when it's someone's deal who wants to sound really in and with it. And not only will weekly poker-with-the-gang sessions destroy your game; they will cost you a lot of friendships. It's practically a rule in those games that all players must lose on alternate Wednesday nights or face expulsion and fines. Failure to give everyone endless chances to get even will make you unpopular with "the guys"—if you're in it for the money, you're going to get banned from the game eventually anyway. So the best course of action is not to play in "friendly" games to begin with, especially since the stakes are seldom high enough to make it worth your while to alienate folks by taking their money. It's fine for you to keep up with your college or high school buddies (who, to a man, will be more worthwhile than anyone you're going to meet in the poker games I'm about to describe), but once you decide to be a serious poker player you should limit your old-buddy contact to happy-hour cocktails and football watching parties. When "the boys" invite you to the weekly game, be busy.

When it comes to finding the right poker games, you're lucky to live in the times that you do. In the decades prior to the 1990s, card rooms run for profit existed in major cities throughout the country, but in nearly every state these games were illegal and therefore dangerous to play in. Hidden poker parlors did business in seedy strip shopping centers where the rents were low or in apartments where adequate security was nigh impossible. Local police had too much crime on their plates to hammer the poker games very often (except in election years, when raids created favorable headlines for political incumbents), but by the same token, law enforcement had no incentive to protect the players. Cheaters thrived in those illegal games. With no state control over the operators, rakes (the part of the pot that goes to the house) were often so high that it was impossible to win regardless of the player's skill level. Many of the people who ran those games were longtime police blotter characters, and robberies at gunpoint during games were common (including one incident in Dallas where the game runner, strapped for cash to the point where he couldn't pay the winners, had his own game hijacked, then later settled his debts to the players with their own money).

Today, things have changed drastically. Some form of gambling is now legal in all but fifteen states, with poker as the next-most common game of chance right behind slot machines. And even if you live in one of those backward areas where gambling is still illegal, there are very few cities in America located more than a three-hour drive from the nearest casino card room. Security is tight around casinos, and players can come and go in absolute safety. Further, the competition from close-by legal operations has even cleaned up the big-city illegal games. Illegal games now go on with competitive rakes to what the casinos charge, and I haven't heard of a single cold-decking (cheating) incident or poker game hijacking in the past ten years or so. In fact, if you're located in one of the cities where poker's still illegal, and where it's difficult to drive to the nearest legal game because of the lack of easy access to and from—New York City with all those tunnels and

New Jersey toll roads to navigate comes to mind, and so do Philadelphia and Pittsburgh—just drop me an e-mail. You're going to have to provide your real name and address, and answer a few questions so that I can verify your identity (and be satisfied that you're not part of the vice squad), but in just a few days' time I'll furnish you a list of the backstreet places to play in your own city, and even give you the name of the person to contact in order to gain entry. This service is free of charge.

Don't be fooled into thinking that just because you're playing in a casino, the game is filled with experts. In every recent ten-handed casino Hold 'Em game I've played in, there have been two or three competent players, and four or five more who think they're experts when really they're not, with the rest of the seats filled by tourists who haven't a clue but have seen the game on television and want to try it out. Today, with the close proximity of poker rooms both legal and otherwise, it's a piece of cake to play in a different place every day, for just about whatever stakes you choose, and still remain relatively anonymous. You simply don't go to the same game more than once a week. You don't play for more than eight hours, and when you're finished, you ride away into the night. You don't go to dinner with poker players, and other than the time spent at the tables, you never see them. You don't inquire into their personal affairs, and you tell them as little about yourself as possible.

Of course, total anonymity is impossible because every game has its nosy people, and in order to keep from alienating the questioners you have to tell them *something*. Always use your real name because your identity is too easy to verify, but don't apply for casino credit or cash any checks because to do either you must give information that you don't want casinos to have; don't accept comped rooms or meals for the same reason. Bring along hundred-dollar bills when you play. When you do drop personal tidbits, say that you have a job, even if you really don't, because in the so-called poker hustlers' world, gainful employment is as much the mark of the sucker as incompetent play. The job should be middle-of-the-road. If you're actually the CEO of Dell, just say that you work in computers and leave the rest to the other players' imagination. And even though playing poker for profit in card rooms is in itself a sort of Walter Mitty existence, don't go overboard with exuberant self-promotion. If you've previously made your living as an auto mechanic, don't try to convince anyone that you're really a Ph.D. in physics because you don't have the knowledge to pull it off. And by the same token, if you really are the Ph.D. and you design nuclear weapons for a living, don't suddenly fulfill your own fantasy and proclaim yourself to be a rodeo cowboy. Be nebulous about your job, but don't claim a profession that you don't fit both in appearance, manner of speaking, and overall knowledge. If anyone asks you for your phone number at work, invent a reason why you can't give it. It usually works to say that your boss is an asshole and won't let you take calls on the job; this will get you out of giving anyone the number and also solidify your image as a worker who's far down on the totem pole.

And as for your skill at playing poker or lack of it—and trust me, they'll all want to know where you learned the game—tell them that you played a lot while growing up, and you're trying to redevelop your chops while working at your job. If you've claimed to have a white-collar job, tell them that you used your poker winnings to pay for some of your college expenses (poker hustlers just *love* the guy who "paid his way through college playing poker" and will just about commit murder in order to give this person a seat at the table). You'll have their mouths watering by the time you're ready to move in for the kill.

Now we've found the game, so let's talk about the image you're going to project. For openers, form a list of behavior patterns that you *don't* want to emulate. Every poker game has regular players, and among them are certain undesirable stereotypes. Putting up with these types is as much a part of playing for profit as developing your own image. You will recognize the following stereotypes within fifteen minutes after sitting down in any game anywhere—trust me, they'll be there—and you should learn to avoid any resemblance to them:

Analytical Man. This guy's usually been to college and speaks in a professsorial tone. He dissects every single hand from start to finish, giving a running commentary on who's probably got what and why they're betting or checking or whatnot, and thinking out loud as he plays his own cards. Usually when the hands are shown at the end, Analytical Man's diatribe is proven wrong, but that doesn't discourage the guy from continuing his commentary. Players react to Analytical Man in varying ways, from mere sniping to the threat of physical violence, but it's best to ignore this guy and treat him as white noise.

Annoying Man. This is the intentionally confrontational man, as opposed to Analytical Man, who is merely stupid and trying to appear intelligent. Annoying Man is normally a better than average player, and his insults are generally directed at other good players in an attempt to throw them off their games. His goal is to make others despise him to the point that they'll play recklessly in an attempt to beat him, and his strategy often works. If you create the impression that you're a poker-playing pigeon you won't have to worry about this guy, because Annoying Man acts as the pigeon's friend and pretends to take the pigeon under his wing. Annoying Man likes to create the impression that it's him and the pigeon against the rest of the players. Rest assured, though, that when he grins at you his real goal is to screw you, and act accordingly. Watch him and learn. Above all, don't imitate any part of the guy.

Chip-Shuffling Man. I think this may be no more than a nervous habit since so many players perform some semblance of chip shuffling, but you should never think that the more expert a man is at dividing his stacks, then shuffling them back together with his index finger, the better player he's going to be. Obviously he's trying to *look* the part of a poker pro, but that doesn't mean that he is one, since his constant chip shuffling indicates only that the guy spends far too much time at the poker or blackjack table practicing. He's like a juggler—really proficient at something that pays absolutely zero. Since he has so much free time, it's a dead cinch that he doesn't have a job and is therefore likely to be an extremely poor credit risk. Don't loan Chip-Shuffling Man any money (you'll be surprised at how soon after making your acquaintance he'll have the nerve to put the touch on you), and above all, don't pick up any of his table habits. If you have to do something with your hands, put them in your pockets and play with your keys and change.

Blindman. That's my personal nickname for the guys with the sunglasses. I think the term originated for me during the time I played with a man who actually was blind, who did wear glasses with black lenses, and who kept his cane under the table and played with a good-looking woman seated near his elbow. When I first sat in on the game I had no idea that the man was handicapped, and thought that the woman constantly whispering in his ear was either giving him playing advice or trying to lure him off to some motel. Later I learned that she was telling him what cards he held and which cards came up on the board. Reflecting back on it, I think that the *real* blindman was a better player than most *pseudo* Blindmen I've run into in casino poker games, and I think that men who have to wear sunglasses and hats pulled low while playing poker are carrying the Walter Mitty bit to a ridiculous degree. If you ask him in private, Blindman will say that he wears the glasses and hat pulled low to eliminate all chance of anyone picking up a tell on him. But as I'll explain in detail in a later chapter, no one can evaluate another player's hand merely from facial expressions, and it's a serious mistake to think someone's a good player just because his eyes are hidden behind blackout lenses like Tom Cruise's in *Collateral*. Blindman thinks he's being really cool and intimidating, when in reality he's making an ass of himself. Never rate anyone's skill by the blackness of his sunglasses, and above all, in your own play leave the shades at home. Golf hats are fine, but keep them tilted back rather than pulling the bill down to hide your eyes.

Funny Man. This guy has a million of 'em, and they're actually hilarious the first time you hear them. In fact, the first time you sit in on the game you're going to wonder how the regular players can keep a straight face with Funny Man around, but in time you'll realize that they've heard all of his stories a thousand times and think he's pretty boring. Funny Man specializes in humorous poker tales. He knows in intimate detail why the starting Hold 'Em hand of ten-deuce is called Doyle Brunson, why two fours is called Doc Nichols, and all about the time that Charley Boyd robbed Everett Goolsby over the telephone (this really happened). Funny Man might or might not be a competent player, and overall he's relatively harmless. The main reason you don't want to emulate Funny Man is that in order to know all these stories, Funny Man has to have spent most of his life sitting around in poker games. Remember, you're a novice. If you have to tell a joke, pick out one that you heard on David Letterman. The other players as a rule don't ever watch Letterman—or anything else on TV other than the sports scores, and then only if they have a bet on some team—so they won't have heard your joke, though many of them will act so cool that they won't laugh at it. The best part is, the fact that you watch Letterman will help classify you as a pigeon in the players' minds, and that's just what you're trying to accomplish.

Desperate Man. Actually this isn't a single man, it's a number of men, and Desperate Man's identity changes from week to week. Desperate Man is the self-proclaimed poker professional who's having a bad run of cards and wants everyone at the table to know about it. What's currently happening to Desperate Man, at least in his own mind, is a thousand times worse than what's ever happened to anyone, and whenever he loses a pot Desperate Man is likely to utter a choking sob. Occasionally when someone draws out on Desperate Man—and I'm not kidding about this—he will get up from the table, march into the restroom, and loudly bang his head against the wall. It never occurs to Desperate Man that losing has destroyed his game and that he could curb his losses by folding a few hands. Desperate Man believes that his play is impeccable just as it's always been. As for Desperate Man's credit worthiness, see the previous remarks about Chip-Shuffling Man. Even though Desperate Man may seem doomed at the moment, the next time you play in the game he may be as happy as a clam. Poker fortunes change, and last week's Desperate Man might be this week's Annoying Man, and vice versa. For obvious reasons, you never want to emulate Desperate Man.

Now you've visited a typical casino poker room game and looked over the personas you *don't* want to assume, so let's talk about the image that you *do* want to project. As for role models in your bearing and demeanor, you can eventually pick your own, but I'm going to suggest someone that it wouldn't hurt to copy.

While many like the cut of Greg Raymer's jib, and while he's truly a perfect gentleman at all times and in all circumstances, Raymer's not your man because he's too self-assured at the poker table. The pigeon should always look slightly confused. Let me tell you about a guy.

I flew into Las Vegas while the 2005 World Series was in progress, and though I never entered a tournament, I did play in quite a few side games. Since I already had it in my mind to write this book, I did something I've never done before and attended the Main Event as one of the railbirds. During the days at the Rio leading up to the finals, and for the brief period downtown at the Horseshoe, I zeroed in on one man. His name is Steve Dannenmann. He's a CPA from Severn, Maryland, and likely you've never heard of him. He was a first-timer in the Main Event, having split his entry fee fifty-fifty with a buddy back home, and in the summer of 2005 he miraculously made it all the way to the final table, finished second, and won over four million dollars. But his success in a single tournament isn't the issue. Since my trip to Las Vegas, I've had a chance to watch the tournament on television, and was glad to see a lot of camera time devoted to Steve Dannenmann and his improbable run to the finals. Do yourself a favor. Tune in to the 2005 World Series on ESPN and get a load of this guy.

At first when he kept surviving daily in the tournament I thought that either Steve Dannenmann had to be for real, or he was performing the greatest hustle in the history of poker, so from the third day on I watched Dannenmann's play very closely. He's for real. Not that he's a poor poker player, because he isn't; he's just not of the caliber required to beat a world-class field like the one he ran into in Las Vegas, and to his credit Dannenmann knew it. He understood perfectly that he was out of his league and played the only way that the Steve Dannenmanns of the world can play in such a tournament and have a chance—tight as a tick, throwing away all but the choicest of starting hands, never bluffing, and hoping for the best. It so happened that for the duration of the tourney the cards ran over Dannenmann, and the rest is, as they say, history.

And talk about your perfect unlikely Main Event finalist!! Steve Dannenmann is clean-shaven, soft-spoken, fresh-faced, with a square-John shortish haircut, and just oozes the part of your basic conservative CPA. He was wide-eyed and in awe of his competition from Day One, never once lost his smile of bewilderment, and spent nearly all of his time during breaks on his cell phone to the folks back home. I'm not kidding; don't miss watching Dannenmann in the 2005 Main Event on ESPN. If there's a must-see for us Pigeons Who Would be Winners, this is the one. If you could somehow bottle Dannenmann's demeanor and attitude and take them home with you, you'd be halfway to the result this book is trying to give before you played a single hand.

But for goodness sake, don't read this chapter, then break out the disguise and try to go around posing as Steve Dannenmann because that won't work. However, if you adopt portions of Dannenmann's persona—or someone else's that you think more in line with your natural image; I'm just using Dannenmann as an example—then alter them to fit into your own personality, you're almost home. Most important, you shouldn't conform to any of the stereotypes described previously, the ones that exist in every casino poker game, because then you'll appear to be a veteran player, and that's just the opposite of what you're trying to achieve. Chip-Shuffling Man doesn't appear to be a pigeon even though he likely is one. You want to *appear* as a pigeon, even though in reality you're something else entirely.

Are you good and bored yet? Well take heart, because in the following chapter we're going to start playing the game. In fact, even as you read this, the people who just don't get it are already pages and pages ahead of you learning when to raise and when to fold. But trust me, some day you'll be glad that you slogged through this chapter, especially when those who just don't get it realize that largely due to the persona you've developed, you play poker at a level that's far above them.

5

The Two-Card Dilemma: To Play or Not to Play, That Is the Question

So now we're ready to discuss playing Texas Hold 'Em in line with the general premise of this book, that is, to play in a manner that disguises the strength of your game. Teaching poker is much tougher than teaching, say, math or history because there is no paint-by-the-numbers, here-you-raise—*click*—and here-you-fold—*click*—method of playing the game. Every decision you make in playing Hold 'Em depends on the strength of your hand, your position relative to the button, your knowledge of the other players' betting habits, and the money you'll risk by betting, calling, or raising versus the amount you'll profit if you win the pot in question. Incidentally, the size of the pot should have influence only before the river card is dealt; if you're obviously and positively beaten after the cards are all out, never call the final bet just because the pot is laying you fifty to one for your money. Nothing you are about to read should be taken as a rule; these are merely guidelines for competent play. And if you think I might be covering my ass in the preceding sentence, you're right, I am. Another good reason for writing this book anonymously is that if you know who I am and happen to turn up in a game where I'm playing, then every time I do something opposed to my own teachings you're going to shout triumphantly, *Wait a minute, that's not what you said to do on page such-and-such.* This is also true with the superstar professionals who've also written books on the subject; if you watch them on TV, you'll see them making plays just the opposite of what their own books teach, and you will see this all the time. Remember, decisions you make at the table will vary depending on the circumstances of the moment, and that's true if you're Johnny Chan, Howard Lederer, Annie Duke, or some yo-yo from Paducah who's just in town for the weekend.

Before I started writing this book I formulated a lesson plan where I'd have separate chapters on (1) before-the-flop play, (2) the play after the flop, (3) action after the turn card, and (4) the play after all the cards are all out. There is a completely different strategy for each of these four parts of the game, so I'm still going to do separate sections on each, but I'm going to break these sections down into one chapter describing really expert play followed by a chapter on the strategy you're going to use to convince these experts that you don't know what you're doing. Additionally, since what you do before the flop invariably affects your play *after* the flop, these different sections are going to overlap some. We're now going to talk about expert before-the-flop strategy, but keep in mind that we're going to have to include some description of after-the-flop examples in order to explain why professionals do some of the things that they do with only two cards in their hand. Confusing? Well, join the crowd; Hold 'Em is a complex game. As you get more familiar through practice and play, the lessons you read here will become clearer to you.

Let's start with an assumption that should really be obvious: Before anyone can disguise their skills at anything, they must have skills to disguise. Therefore, since we're talking about poker, before you can make plays that look as if you don't know what you're doing, you must first know how a player who *does* know what he's doing would perform in the same situation.

There is no better way to disguise your skills in Hold 'Em than to make before-the-flop decisions that look wrong, but in reality are executed perfectly, because for reasons that hold no water whatsoever, most of these so-called experts rate their opponents' play mainly by the two pocket cards that the opponent shows down after all the bets are in. Show down an inferior two-card hand—especially one where you've drawn out on one of the experts to win a pot—and the hotshots will rate you as a sucker right away. In this chapter and the one to follow, we're going to learn how to play weak two-card hands occasionally without giving away the farm.

I think that this obsession with starting hands comes from reading a book that nearly all serious Hold 'Em players have just about committed to memory, *Texas Hold 'Em* by David Sklansky, published in the middle 1970s. The book was the first to rate opening two-card hands in the order of their strength, doing so through a series of charts that show, from strongest to weakest, the rank of every possible two-card Hold 'Em hand. In addition to ranking hands, Sklansky also instructs players which of these two-card combinations to play and which ones to fold, depending on the player's position in the hand relative to the button.

(*Note:* Most books on Hold 'Em, including Sklansky's, also include rudimentary instructions on the basic rules of the game. Countless gallons of ink get wasted in explaining how hands are dealt, how and when the button is moved, how the betting proceeds before and after the flop, and most of these books also include a lengthy list of Hold 'Em terms and definitions at some point. Personally, I think this sort of information is provided because the writer is afraid that prospective readers won't fork over the purchase price unless his book contains enough pages, and therefore includes a lot of filler material. I rate this sort of information as equivalent to, say, a football coach who's writing a book on strategy in the red zone, yet starts out with explanations of the length of the field, the kickoff, how many players are on each team, and how to make a first down. I don't believe that anyone interested enough in poker to read this book doesn't already know the rules of Hold 'Em and hasn't at least watched the game on television. With that in mind, I've eliminated pedestrian instruction in an effort to keep from boring you. If you're the one-in-a-thousand reader who doesn't know the definitions of the flop, the button, the turn card, the river card, etc., etc., etc., you should set this book aside right now, go read up on the rudiments of the game, and come back to us when you have.)

Sklansky's *Texas Hold 'Em* is without question the definitive work on the game, particularly the limit poker form, and even after thirty-odd years in print it's got more accurate info than anything ever written on the subject. (Here I nearly added "except for this one" but decided to let you judge for yourself after putting both methods into practice.) There is, however, a drawback to relying exclusively on Sklansky's methods. Back in the 1970s and '80s, I played a great deal of poker with Sklansky himself, downtown at the ten-and-twenty table in the Golden Nugget's card room, and I was amazed at the consistency with which Sklansky beat the game. The guy never seemed to lose, and one day at lunch I remarked to Junior Hess—in my estimation one of the three finest limit poker players I've ever met, and another man you'll never see on television—that I felt equal in skill to just about every player at the table, but that Sklansky was the one man I couldn't beat and had just about given up trying to. Junior seemed lost in thought, as if he couldn't make up his mind whether to share his secret, then leaned closer and half whispered, "If you want to play Sklansky, just read his book." I grilled Junior at length on what he meant by that statement, but he'd said all he was going to say. When we finished eating, he didn't complain when I picked up the tab.

The very next day I went downtown to the Gamblers' Book Store, bought a copy of Sklansky's *Texas Hold 'Em*, and stayed up all night reading every word. And guess what—Junior Hess was exactly right. Anyone reading Sklansky's book and learning its contents could quickly see that Sklansky played exactly the way his book instructed, so thereafter I always knew Sklansky's hand by his position relative to the button and whether or not he'd raised before the flop, and if I didn't have Sklansky beat I simply threw my hand away. I don't think I ever lost another pot to the guy. Whether you follow someone's teachings, no matter whose they are or whether you're the school-of-hard-knocks type who learns the game strictly through experience, if you are to be successful you must play in accordance with this basic assumption: *To win consistently at Texas Hold 'Em, you must **alter your style of play**.* I've watched Sklansky on television in the past couple of years and noted that he alters his style much more effectively than he did in the old days. He was a great player then, and a quarter century of experience has done nothing but make him even more formidable.

The preceding anecdote also doesn't change the fact that Sklansky's book is the one work dealing with limit Hold 'Em that all players should read. In my early days of playing, I heard a great deal of table-talk debate over which two-card hand was the best hand to have before the flop, and while I never bought into the myth that jack-ten suited was the best because of all the straight and flush possibilities, I confess that I did waste a lot of time going over the debated points in my mind. David Sklansky's book offered the following quotation on the subject: "Two aces is the best hand, period." I'll never forget reading that sentence. After all the debate over the best starting hand I'd heard, there was the answer in black and white. Two aces. Christ, *finally*, there it was. My palms were suddenly damp.

But now, over a quarter of a century later, I've got to make the following observation: In all due respect, Mr. Sklansky, and in the lingo of my teenage niece, Well, *duh*-uh. Please name any poker game, draw or stud, other than low ball, where two wired aces *isn't* the best starting hand possible. You can't. As far as I'm concerned, now that I'm armed with decades of experience to look back on, Sklansky might as well have announced that the world was round.

Having said that, I'll also state that if you play Hold 'Em according to Sklansky and the cards break even, you're going to win in the long run. But if you're playing with professsionals or top-flight amateurs, you're just not going to win very much. Good players will quickly figure out that you're playing according to Sklansky, and thereafter they'll fold whenever you bet unless they've got you beat. You'll pocket a lot of blinds and after-the-flop money, but if good players stay with you until the end of the hand, more often than not they're going to beat you. With the methods I'm proposing here no one's going to realize that you're an expert, and, when you've got a really big-time hand, even the pros at the table are going to pay you off like slot machines.

In Sklansky's book, after the definitive "two-aces-are-the-best-hand" statement, there follows a chart giving the rank of various hands (the best after AA being KK, the next-best after KK being AK, and so on and so forth) and also telling you with which of these hands you should see the flop depending on your position relative to the button, and when you should raise before the flop and when you should merely call. Modern hand evaluations come from a computer's lightning calculation of every possible combination of five cards that can come on the board after removing the two cards in question from the deck, and then figuring out which two-card hands will win the greatest percentage of the time. Considering that Sklansky wrote his book prior to the modern computer age, it is stunning that if a modern computer's ranking of hands is compared with his ranking, the differences are few and far between.

But now, having praised Sklansky's ranking of hands to high heaven, I'm going to take the first step in contradicting the Las Vegas crowd by giving you my own take on all of this two-card hand evaluation: *If you memorize the ranking of every possible two-card hand, and every two-card hand's chances of beating every **other** two-card hand, your head will be filled with such a boondoggle of useless information that you'll never learn to play the game.*

Look. Knowing which two cards are favored over which *other* two cards makes for great conversation *after* the cards are all out and the hands showed down, but in order for this sort of knowledge to assist you in making decisions while playing, you'd have to know all the other players' hands as well as your own. And if I'm playing in any game where the players always know their chances of beating the two-card hand I hold *before* I show my cards, then I'm examining the deck with a microscope!

So now, once and for all, here's the Poker Pigeon's evaluation of two-card starting Hold 'Em hands, boiled down to a single sentence: **The best possible two-card hand in limit Texas Hold 'Em is the one that best matches up with the cards dealt face-up on the flop.** And in line with that statement, here's one that I consider even more important: **Before-the-flop play is about 5 percent responsible for whether you win or lose in the long run, while the other 95 percent of your success in Hold 'Em depends on how you play your hand** *after the flop.* That's it. You don't get a chart of hand rankings here because I'm not going to furnish one—but don't feel cheated. If I gotta make my book thicker, I'm gonna do it with funny stories and compelling dialogue.

After reading my definitive statement on the ranking of Hold 'Em hands, it's now your turn to stand in unison and shout, "Well, *duh*-uh." Sklansky's voice in saying this will probably be the loudest of all. The fact that the best hand is the one that the flop hits on the nose is something any moron should know, but please hear me out. We're about to discuss the way to win a few pots with inferior two-card hands and drive the poker wizards up the wall but have them drooling to play some more hands against you.

Notice I haven't said that AA, KK, or AK aren't hands you should play aggressively before the flop—because they are. If you get one of those three hands you should use up all the raises possible in order to make players with inferior cards toss them in, thus giving your strong hand a better chance of winning the pot, but in limit poker you're not going to chase nearly as many hands with pre-flop raises as you are in no-limit. In fact, depending on your position, your raises very well may not eliminate *anyone*. Your best raising position is the first seat to the left of the big blind because your raise is going to force everyone to pay double *all at once* to see the flop (as opposed to the situation where the player calls the big blind, someone raises behind him, and then he has to call an additional amount on the second time around), so you're likely to chase a few players that might look at the flop otherwise. But in late position, or in the big or small blind position, forget it; everyone who's already called the big blind, when faced with putting an additional amount equal to another big blind in the pot, will come in every single time. Experts all understand this, and sometimes will not raise before the flop even if they hold AA, so that their hand will be well disguised and they might catch a few fish that they wouldn't otherwise.

Always keep the following in mind: If you hold two pocket

aces, then you are a prohibitive head-up favorite over any other two-card hand. However, if four or more players are in the pot opposing you, then you have become an *underdog to the field*, meaning that your chances of beating *all four* opponents are less than fifty percent. In other words, even if you hold the best two-card hand possible, you'll generally win the pot in limit Hold 'Em less than half of the time where there are five players seeing the flop.

Even more discouraging to the player who sits around waiting for a monster two-card starting hand before he'll come into a pot is the risk/reward factor. If your strong two-card hand holds up and you do take the pot, you're not going to win as much money as you're going to lose if someone beats you. Or better put, here's another of the Poker Pigeon's declarations for posterity: **Limit Texas Hold 'Em is a game where the superior player will come out ahead in the long run, but it's also a game where a player who thinks he's good but in truth is merely a tightass cannot possibly win.** Experts (and what book writer *isn't* an expert?) describe the most effective play as tight but aggressive. I agree, but also expand the definition. I preach tight and aggressive, *but also loose and aggressive at certain strategic times.*

With regard to your anticipated success in playing only the premium two-card hands, let's say you're in a ten-and-twenty game where the blinds are five and ten dollars, which is the current structure in just about all casino poker games—the small and big blinds are always one fourth and one half of the maximum bet, respectively. You have the button, meaning that you have the last action, and after three players have called the big blind in front of you, you look down to find two lovely red aces in your hand. Naturally you raise the initial bet from ten to twenty dollars. More than half the time the person to your left, having already been forced to put in five dollars as the small blind, will risk fifteen dollars more in order to see the flop. The person having the big blind, whose price to play is a mere additional ten dollars, will call over *80* percent of the time. (This is true only if you're playing with mortals; really fine players and Sklansky disciples will fold their hands in the two blind positions unless their cards are really strong. According to Sklansky, if your hand in the big blind position is less than AA, KK, or AK, you should throw it away whenever there's a raise, and in the *small* blind position you shouldn't even risk the amount required to equal the big blind.) In the case at hand, where you hold two aces on the button, everyone who's already called the big blind will see your raise, so you'll go to the flop with a hundred and twenty bucks in the pot, twenty of which is your own money, and there'll be five players opposing you.

Are you beginning to see where I'm coming from?

If the other players fail to pair or pick up a draw on the flop, they're going to check to you. You're naturally going to bet, and at that point the other players will all throw their hands away. You'll drag the before-the-flop action and show a hundred-dollar profit. Congratulations.

But let's say that in the case of two of the players you're up against, one holds the 78 of spades and the other's hand is K10 in two different suits. The flop produces the 9 of spades, the 10 of hearts, and the 4 of spades. The players who've caught nothing will fold at the first bet made, leaving you alone against the 78 and the K10 off-suit. You're still in the lead with your pair of aces, but how do you like your chances of winning the pot against the two people remaining? The first player has both an open-ended straight draw (any jack or any six—a total of eight of the cards remaining in the deck, will make his hand) and a flush draw (any spade—and there are seven of those left besides the six and jack of spades, which are both included in the cards that will fill the player's straight), so if any one of fifteen cards is among the final two to be dealt, that player wins the pot.

But even worse for you, the player with the K10 has picked up a pair of tens on the flop, so *that* opponent will beat you with any king or any ten unless the king or ten happens to be a spade, in which event Player One will make his flush. There is one non-spade 10 left in the deck along with two nonspade kings, so Player Number Two has three cards left to beat you with, which, added to the fifteen cards that win for Player One, means that if any one of *eighteen* cards hits the board among the final two, then you are going to finish with empty pockets.

Now how are your aces doing?

Later on in the book we'll have a session on figuring the odds for and against making draws once the flop has appeared, but for now you'll have to take my word for the fact that the chances of one of these players beating your two aces are almost *three to one against you*.

Of course, you don't know what the other players are holding. You're still in the lead and, after the player with the K10 makes his token high-pair ten-dollar bet after the flop, you're going to raise. Now you've shoveled an additional twenty bucks into the pot. On the turn card you'll bet twenty more, but after the river card (if you're still winning) you'll have to forgo the final bet and show your hand down (or if you *do* go ahead and bet, both other players, having missed their draws, will fold—so okay, the guy with the K10 might pay you off, but if he's a good player and you've represented your high pocket pair well enough, he'll fold if he doesn't improve). So if your two aces stand up against the odds, you're going to win about eighty bucks in addition to the pre-flop action, or a total of $180.

And if the odds win out and you lose with your aces? Well, whenever one of the other players draws out on you, you're going to have to stand a twenty-dollar raise, so if you stay in to the end you will lose about a hundred bucks more than you've put in prior to the flop. So you stand to win $180 and lose $120, a payoff of three to two on your money, when the odds against you after the flop are about *three to one*. If you play a thousand pots like this one, plan on returning very quickly from being an aspiring poker professional to being a working stiff. I think Doyle Brunson probably puts it best in his book on the power system: The three so-called best starting hands will win small pots when they stand up but lose large pots when they don't.

(Here the no-limit guys will shout in unison, "See there. That's why we're playing in the big-time, where you can **protect your fuckin' hand**." And it's true that where you can bet big before the flop, you will seldom see more than one player up against you, and your pair of aces will be a much bigger favorite to win. But in limit poker, when your big hand gets beat, you won't lose so much that you can't survive to play some more. In no-limit, however, the one time in four that your pair of aces fails to win in head-up play is likely going to cripple you. In limit poker the percentages will work for you in the long run, if you're a superior player, but one short-term loss in a no-limit game can send you packing.)

Which brings us to another Postulate from the Poker Pigeon: **The most important step in learning to play AA, KK, or AK is knowing when to throw those hands away.**

Fact: Any jackass can take two aces and raise the maximum possible before the flop, but just because you've got money invested, there is no rule that says you have to stay in the pot till the bitter end, when it's obvious that you're beat. It's amazing how many otherwise competent Hold 'Em players never learn this, continuing to throw good money after bad so that, when their big starting hands lose in the end, they can turn up their two aces and moan about God being against them even though they're not going to garner a smidgen of sympathy from anyone at the table. If you're paying attention, you can tell when you're beat and, either on the turn or the river, you will save yourself somewhere between forty and sixty bucks a hand in a ten-and-twenty game by folding. In an eight-hour poker session this situation will come up multiple times, so you could save yourself as much as *three hundred bucks* per session merely by not keeping 'em honest at the end. Worth looking into, huh? Of course, there will be times when you'll fold the best hand and feel foolish for doing so, but not calling weaker players' check-raises on the end or throwing away two aces when the pot gets double-raised on the turn will save you a lot of money in the long run.

Since I've now dissed the three best starting hands in Hold 'Em, you're probably wondering what starting hands this moron is going to say that you *should* feel confident with. I'll get to that, but first I'm going to give you the Poker Pigeon's list of hands that you should *never* play when you must stand a raise before the flop. Color these two-card combinations *terrible*, and I think that most people will find a few surprises here.

The Absolutely Terrible Two-Card Hands that the Poker Pigeon *never* plays in early position if there is a raise before the flop: KQ, KJ, K10, AJ, A10—or ace-anything other than AK or AQ. You're now going to think, *Wait a minute, I saw Johnny Lederer (or Howard Chan, one of those marquee guys) come in with KQ in the Superstars Invitational and win a pot that a show dog couldn't jump over.* Yes, you did, but please go back to the comments about television play on pages 5–6 of this book, and remember the differences between no-limit tournament strategy and limit cash-game play. The superstar who played KQ on television was in a situation where the size of the blinds forces one to play more hands than in a cash game and, furthermore, causes players to raise on pre-flop hands that in a cash game, they'd probably throw away. In that situation, even if the pot is raised before the flop, KQ is likely to be the best hand.

In a limit game, however, the hands listed in the preceding paragraph are *almost never* the best hand in a raised pot, and furthermore are likely to cost the player a ton if he plays any of them. The secret to winning in limit Hold 'Em isn't necessarily taking down a lot of pots, even though that certainly helps. Holding your losses down to a minimum in pots that you don't win is at least as important if not more so.

Take KQ, a holding that at first glance looks like a great big starting hand. In a pot raised before the flop, you're probably up against a hand that contains an ace, probably AK or AQ, or a medium pair at the minimum, 10s or higher. Guess what. Your KQ is an underdog to any of these hands, and not only that— some of the other players who hang around for the flop are almost sure to have either an ace or a pair as well, so you might be seriously behind three or four players going in. Unless you get a miracle flop, such as J,10,9, any card on the board that pairs you is likely to cost you dearly. If you catch a king, AA beats you and so do AK and KK, and if you catch a queen you're a loser to AA, KK, AQ and QQ as well. If you're in early position, since you've paired the highest card on the board, you're going to have to bet, and you're probably tossing manure at the fan, which is going to come back in your face very shortly. Sure, you will win a few pots with KQ in early position, just as you might win with any other two-card hand, but the chances of your losing even if you hit one of your hole cards is much greater than if you came in with, say, 10-9. With 10-9, if the biggest card on the flop happens to be a 10, then you're much more likely to have a winner.

Believe it or not, I'd even prefer *72* over KQ in a pot raised before the flop, and while we wait a minute for the giggles to subside, I'll explain myself. Yeah, yeah, I know, 72 off-suit, worst hand in Hold 'Em, tee-hee—nobody comes in with that hand other than a fool. Well, *I'll absolutely guarantee you that against AK, KK, AK, AQ, or QQ, 72 will win more pots than KQ, hands down*. Plus, if you catch nothing on the flop to go with 72, you can get quickly away from the hand, but if something comes out to match KQ and you're up against one of the four hands just mentioned, you will be forced to bet when in fact you are almost drawing dead. Not that I'm recommending playing seven-deuce, either, but I'm just making a point here.

Note that I make no distinction between suited starting hands and *un*suited starting hands. One of the major mistakes I see, even in seasoned professionals, is playing a hand just because it's suited when you wouldn't play the identically ranked two cards if they were of different suits. Oddly enough, you will make a flush only about *three percent* more often with suited cards than you will with unsuited cards. The next time you play, keep track of how many times three cards of a suit come on the board, versus the number of times when *four* cards of a suit appear. There won't be nearly as much difference as you think.

Players most often make the mistake of coming into pots with weak hands just because they're suited when the suited hand contains an ace and a small card, say 6 or 7. If you play this hand and make an ace-high flush, well and good, but where are you going to be if an ace hits the board? You're going to be up against an ace with a better kicker than yours, is where, and unless you make a near impossible draw-out, you're going to lose your ass in the pot. As always, I know that players at the final table in the World Series will play ace-anything suited, and act as if A9 is the pure nuts going in, but if you want to be a consistent winner in limit poker, *don't you do it*. Those hands are absolute killers for the player holding them when an ace hits the board, so much so that ace–little suited will cost players many times more than they will ever win with the hand. Once and for all:

Don't play hands merely because they contain suited cards. Do play suited cards where you can make a straight *or* a flush, and there'll be more along that line in a page or so.

We just dealt with KQ, and I'm not going to give any examples relating to KJ, K10, AJ, or A10. The reason for not playing these cards in early position, when the pot is raised before the flop, is exactly the same as with KQ: if there is a raise, the raiser likely has either a large or medium pair or one card that's equal to one of yours to go along with a bigger kicker, and you are almost certainly far behind going in.

Now I'm going to turn you around a little bit. In *late* position where you have KQ, KJ, K10, AJ, or A10, and no one has raised before the flop when it's your turn, *that's when you should raise with these hands.* For current and future reference, when I say late position I mean *on the button or in one of the two seats directly to the right of the button.* And yes, I know that some books define early, late, and middle positions, but I don't. There are three seats at the table that I consider late position; all other seats I define as *early* position. Later on we're going to get extensively into the importance of position and how it affects your play (and why I don't think position is near as important as most poker pros will tell you), but for now, let's just leave it that *the later your position, the weaker the pre-flop hands it is permissible for you to play.* While in early position you shouldn't play the above five hands in a raised pot; in *late* position, if no one has raised by the time the action gets around to you, you have what is almost certainly the best hand on the board. The most absolute, unbreakable rule in Hold 'Em (and the rule that I'll no doubt suggest you ignore within the next few chapters) is, *never give anyone a free ride when you've got them beat, because doing so will get you drawn out on.* If you think you have the best hand before the flop, or at any other point in a hand, raise. Always.

In fact, when you have the first chair to the right of the button, and four or more players have come in the pot before you, you should probably raise occasionally *no matter what two cards you have*, in an effort to steal the button. "Stealing the button" means forcing the player who has the button to fold, thus leaving you with last action throughout the hand. The ploy I've just described is actually pretty advanced, though not one in a hundred players will recognize it as such. And after you've stolen the button with some two-card piece-of-shit hand such as J4, and the cards happen to fall for you and you win a pot, everyone other than the really skilled players at the table are going to think, "What a *pigeon*, man," and you'll be on the road to creating just the image you're trying to.

So, what hands (other than the obvious AA, KK, or AK, of course) should we play in early position? Well, even though many of the big boys don't advocate it, I recommend that you look at the flop with suited connectors (cards with which you can make either a flush or a straight) no matter what position you're sitting in, if you only have to call one raise to jump in there (in cases where there are multiple raises you should toss suited connectors in unless there are five or more players in the pot). Your goal in playing suited connectors is to make straights or flushes, and if you do make your hand, it really doesn't make any difference in what position you're sitting (position does make a difference when you're *drawing* for a straight or flush, as opposed to situations where your hand is already made, because there are certain tricks you can pull after the flop to get free draws after the turn, but those are advanced moves that a pigeon shouldn't know and that, therefore, you shouldn't practice). You should never play cards that fit only *both ends* of a straight (such as 6-10), or cards where there are two blank spaces in between (one blank space is fine; in other words, it's fine to play 79 suited, while 69 should go to the center of the table with the rest of the discards). We used to call suited connectors with two or three blank spaces in between "grasshopper connectors." You don't want to play grasshopper connectors because so few combinations will fit to make your straight (with the aforementioned 6-10, for example, only 789 will make a straight, while with, say, 9, 10, there are four combinations that will stretch). In order to win at limit Hold 'Em you must make straights and flushes, and playing hands that can fit into both is a big, big deal.

Now we'll talk about small-to-medium pairs, say any pair smaller than 10s. Most people play any and all pairs, though in my opinion this is a mistake. Where your pair is 9s or lower, it's almost three to one that at least one card higher than your pair will appear on the flop, and when that happens you must either fold your hand or chase a pot where someone else takes the betting lead and hope that they are bluffing or that your own hand will improve on the turn or on the river. Either of the latter two choices is lousy play, and there will be an extensive explanation of why later on.

"But hold it," you say, "what about the possibility of your making a set, where a card equal to your pair comes out on the flop and you have a hidden three-of-a-kind? Sets are the absolute berries, man, and that's why you gotta play them pairs."

Yeah, okay, let's talk about sets. As I've said before, there will be a complete discussion on figuring mathematical probabilities in Hold 'Em in a later chapter, so for now, take my word that your chances of making a set on the flop are six in fifty, or just slightly more than seven to one against you. Even if we accept the theory that the pot you'll win with a set will be bigger than the normal pot because your three-of-a-kind is hidden, you should never play with a small-to-medium pair unless the pot is laying you at least five to one for your money, and even then you should toss in the hand immediately after the flop unless (1) you do make your set or (2) no card bigger than your pair shows on the flop. Also, unless the board pairs and you make a full house with your set, in about one out of every five hands your set will lose to a straight or flush.

Folding small to medium pairs before the flop is a difficult but necessary part of learning to play Hold 'Em at a higher level. You can heed my advice here or you can tell me I'm full of it and play those small pairs until the cows come home. As always, it's your money, and I confess that having a 3 hit the board to go with the pair of 3s in your hand is a feeling akin to orgasm. But if you continue to play small pairs where there are less than five players in the pot, you will come out on the short end of the stick in the long run—and if you look me up after you've played Hold 'Em consistently for, say, ten years, I'll be happy to say that I told you so.

Here I should point out that when you fold a small to medium pair, you should never let the other players know that you're doing so. Folding pairs will raise eyebrows all around the table, and will cause the really top-flight players to realize that there is more to your game than meets the eye. Along the same lines, even though you'll see players on television showing bluffs after their opponents have folded (their general reason for doing this is "for advertisement," though I believe that they are really so bursting with pride over bluffing successfully that they gotta show the world), you should never show your cards to anyone unless you are required to. Remember, you're too dumb to bluff, and bluffing in limit poker is generally a waste of time anyway.

There is one exception to the never-showing-your-cards rule, and I suppose this is as good a lead-in as any to the meat of our discussion, which is how to go about disguising your poker skills. Occasionally, you should come into a pot with really weak cards (J3 or 10-2 or 94 or . . . well, you get the idea), and when you fold after looking at the flop, "accidentally" turn your cards up. This move should look clumsy and takes a little practice—I generally start to toss in my hand in the conventional manner, and then "accidentally" strike my cards in midair with a trailing fore-finger. All card room rules require that, when a player's cards are exposed, the dealer must turn the two exposed cards faceup in the center so that everyone can have a look at them. And trust me, whenever you do this, every player at the table will take notice. This maneuver will cost you a little pre-flop money, but the cost will be nothing compared to the future payoff you'll receive when you do come up with a hand (and before you ask, accidentally-on-purpose showing your folded hand isn't cheating; in fact, the poker hustlers will just *love* to look at your folded hands and will believe that you're stupid for letting it happen).

Now it's time to take up the subject of playing a few bad hands in such a way that the cost is minimal and so that you'll even win a few pots with cards that an idiot wouldn't play. It's not hard to pick out the bad hands, but the trick is to learn to play these cards but not lose much with them, as discussed in the next chapter. That's right. In the chapter coming up we begin learning how to play poker like a pigeon but take the money home.

See you on the next page. I'm looking forward to it, and hope that you are as well.

6

Playing Bad Hands Well

or,
Starting Out with Shit, but Coming Up Roses

Okay, now you're ready to roll. You've found the right game and developed your own mild-mannered, Steve Dannenmann-like personality. You've read the opening chapters of this book and have boned up on Sklansky, and have a pretty good idea of how the experts play—though it isn't a requirement that you have expert play *down to a T*; remember that this isn't Las Vegas, and your competition isn't as stiff as it would be out in the desert. You're ready now to inject a few pigeon moves into your play, enough to fool the opposition into thinking that you have feathers and wings and such.

So *now* what?

A word of caution: You must be careful not to fall into the rut of playing bad hands too often, because then the exposed weaknesses in your game will be real instead of counterfeit. Most of the time, say, 95 percent, you're going to play according to Sklansky (today's Sklansky, not the Sklansky from thirty years ago); it's just that on occasion you're going to slip, and—to all outward appearance at any rate—slip badly. And when you do slip the other players are going to know about it, and the times that you slip are going to cause them to rate your style of play as exceptionally poor.

As I said earlier, the primary indicator that other players will use in evaluating you is the strength of the two cards in your hand. There are other meters to show your skill or lack of it, moves that occur after the flop such as the weak players' check-raise, the failure to play your good hands aggressively, the handing out of free cards when it's obvious that others are drawing to beat you, the chasing of obviously better hands after the flop with second or third pair, and numerous other indicators. In future chapters we'll discuss these other ineptitudes and how to inject them occasionally into your play. But for now let's stick to coming into the occasional pot with a weak starting hand, and how to avoid giving the ranch away while doing so.

As usual we'll begin with an assumption, as follows: **Poor Texas Hold 'Em players lose only a small portion of their money by starting out with weak two-card hands. The bulk of the inept players' losses are due to a combination of the following: starting out weak, catching mere pieces of the flop, and instead of folding when they should, drawing obsessively against obviously superior hands to the bitter end.** Occasionally, of course, the weak draw out on the strong, but never often enough to make winners out of losers.

In the previous chapter we learned of the starting hands (A10, KQ, etc.) that you should *never* play in early position and the reasons for throwing them away, i.e., that even if the flop hits these hands, the player holding them is going to lose in the long run. So carrying that premise a step farther, let's look at a few really poor hands that it's all right to play occasionally in line with the illusion we're trying to create, because if the flop hits *these* hands in certain ways, you'll nearly always win.

Enough talk, let's go. You're in a ten-and-twenty game, either in a casino or backstreet card room, grinning stupidly around you at the self-imagined poker sharks. The first few times around the table you play 'em close to the vest, entering pots with only primo starting hands and playing to the end only when you've got a legitimate shot to win. Finally a hand comes up where you're in the big blind, and you look down to see the 10 of diamonds and the 4 of clubs in your hand. There are only two callers before the button, and the player on the button raises. The small blind throws his hand away.

You squint once again at your 10-4, assume a sort of dreamy look, and toss another ten bucks into the pot (and yes, your expression when calling is important; remember, just like the fake handoff on a play-action pass, you gotta sell your maneuver so that the linebackers will be crashing the gaps when you're ready to toss one over their heads). You might even consider flapping your wings and pecking around for kernels of corn on the floor, but that might cause the casino personnel to call the guys with the butterfly nets. The two remaining players call the raise as well. The dealer then knocks on the table, burns one card, and produces a flop consisting of A,10,9.

What you do here is check and, if anyone behind you bets, you throw your hand away. You might want to try the accidental-on-purpose card exposure trick to show the others what a lunkhead they're up against, but above all, do not waste a penny more than the twenty bucks you've already squandered.

"But wait a minute," you shout, "you had a pair. That ten hit you right in the old bread basket."

Yeah, sure.

But listen. Playing something like 10-4 in early position gets really tricky when the flop does happen to sort of hit your hand, like the pair of 10s you've made in this case. A legitimately poor player (as opposed to someone trying to *look* like an inferior player) would bet his pair immediately and, if no one raised behind him, assume that his pair of 10s was the best hand at that point, and continue to bet throughout the hand. It would never occur to Ol' Fogbrain that someone who calls behind him likely has a 10 with a better kicker than his, a pocket pair higher than 10s, an ace with a small kicker, or at the very least a QJ, giving him an open-ended straight draw. If Fogbrain isn't already beaten, any card bigger than his ten that comes up on the turn or the river is going to beat him. Instead of wasting only ten bucks to see the flop, as in the case of the Imitation Pigeon—you—Fogbrain is going to throw away an additional forty or fifty testing the water. Every once in a while Fogbrain will catch a 4 or another 10 on the turn or river and win the pot, but in the long run he's going to have to own a bank or a few producing oil rigs in order to stay in action.

Of course if the flop misses your hand entirely (AAK or something similar) you throw the hand away just as you would with A,10,9 on the board. Even Ol' Fogbrain could figure that one out.

But now here's the postulate that's really the secret to playing like a pigeon but taking the money home: **When you come into a pot with really weak cards, don't go any further than the flop unless the flop hits you** *in at least two places.*

And this happens a whole lot more often than one would think. Peek ahead at the chapter titled "The Oddball Odds of Texas Hold 'Em" if you want, or just take my word for now that when playing 10-4, the odds against catching two 10s, two 4s, or a 10 *and* a 4 on the flop are just a hair more than thirteen to one. So if you come into a pot with weak cards fifteen times during a four-hour poker session, the odds are strong that the flop is going to hit you in at least two places one or two of those times. Those are the pots that you'll likely win with weak starting hands in early position, and when you show your 10-4 or J2 or whatever on the end, you're also going to send Desperate Man into the john for a head-banging session. Further, if you win *only* *one* of those fifteen pots, you're not going to lose any money to speak of with weak starting hands, and when you do make good hands with good cards, the other players will refuse to believe that you have anything and therefore pay you off with mountains of chips.

It works. Believe it or not, it really does. If you catch a 10 *and* a 4 on the flop to go with your 10-4, or—even better—*two* 4s or *two* 10s, then you've gone from being a massive underdog to a heavy favorite in the hand. And when you proudly display your 10-4 off-suit and scoop in the pot from your big blind position, wait till you hear the moans and groans. Conversely, if you play really unlucky in a session and *never* catch a flop to go with your weak starting hand, if you throw the hands away after the flop you'll be out only ten or so bucks per hand, less than two hundred dollars in a ten-and-twenty game, and that's chicken feed compared with what you'll win when you catch a few cards. In the same situation a really poor player would lose between *forty* and *sixty* dollars per weak starting hand, or from two to four hundred more than you're going to lose in the same period of time. Limit poker adds up. Trust me.

Oh, and one more word of caution. Play those weak hands only in early position, because your purpose in coming into pots with 10-4s and whatnot is to create an illusion. Expert players will occasionally play weak hands in *late* position (operating under the theory that with last action they have a great advantage if the flop hits their hand; frankly, I don't subscribe to the late-position theory nearly as strongly as the pseudo-professionals of the world, and I believe that position matters a great deal more when you're on a draw than it does when you already have a hand), so if you flash your 10-4 when you're on the button, they're not going to think your play is near as horrible as you want them to. As I said before we'll go into position play in great detail later on, so hopefully, when you get to that section, the tip I'm throwing out in this paragraph will be clearer to you.

Finally (and this is what puts you miles ahead of the don't-get-its who skipped the chapter on bearing and demeanor), when you do take down pots with really crappy hands in early position, never yield to the temptation to act smug about it. You should prepare yourself for the ridicule that the experts are going to send your way (and boy, are you ever in for some) and the tongue-lashings you'll get from Desperate Man and Analytical Man over your choices of starting hands, but *don't let it affect you*. Never apologize to anyone for winning a pot with weak cards, because you're a pigeon and don't know weak cards from sic 'em.

For examples on how *not* to act after winning a pot with two cards that Charley the Bulldog wouldn't play, just tune in to the World Series on ESPN. There you'll see the guy being drawn out on throwing a fit (think Hellmuth) and screaming over what a moron his opponent happens to be, and that's just the reaction you'll be looking for from Desperate Man and his cronies. But the World Series participant who's done the drawing out will often show his own ass by *arguing* with the so-called expert and explaining why the play he's just made isn't nearly as bad as it looks, and *his* actions here show even less class than the guy doling out the tongue-lashing. Chalk that sort of behavior up to the premise that the guy who's just drawn out on the expert would *rather lose money* than be thought of as an inferior player, and believe it or not, that's just the way that the would-be television stars participating in the World Series of Poker secretly feel. Remember, as the resident pigeon you're not even smart enough to argue, so you should greet all tongue-lashings with expressions of total puzzlement, and continue to look dazed and confused right up to the point that you get up from the table and take the money home.

Before we go on to a few suggestions on how to play hands after the flop, I think we should now slip in the chapter on figuring odds peculiar to Texas Hold 'Em because the ability to calculate your chances of hitting this hand or that hand will determine the decisions you make once the flop hits the table. So here the math lesson comes, and you may now get out your legal pads to use as work sheets. Or if math bores you to tears, you can skip the next chapter and take your place alongside the don't-get-its of the world. Make no mistake: I think you'll be screwing up badly if you don't pay careful attention to the next few pages, but as with everything else in this book, what you want to learn is entirely up to you.

7

The Oddball Odds of Texas

Remember John Nash? He was the guy that Russell Crowe played in *A Beautiful Mind*, the one who wrote near-indecipherable equations on the inside of his dormitory window at Princeton. The equations, complete with x's, y's, mile-long fractions, and parentheses two- and three-lines high, were strung out from one pane of glass to another and stretched from ceiling to sill. Nash tried for months to solve one problem without ever reaching a solution, and finally hauled his desk over to the window in frustration. With his roommate—a guy who, it turned out later, was really a figment of Nash's imagination—helping out, he then hoisted the heavy piece of furniture over the sill to crash into kindling wood two stories below. Students crossing the ground-level courtyard stopped in their tracks to gape and whisper among themselves.

Over the years to follow, John Nash developed lots and lots of imaginary friends to go with the desk-tossing roommate and wound up writing his equations on the walls at various insane asylums where he was an inmate. Christ, the guy even saw little people in the periphery of his vision fifty years later, right after

the Nobel Prize. While neither the movie nor the book
on giving a definitive reason for Nash's mental break-
, I believe that he was a genius of the first order who al-
ed high-level mathematics to drive him nuts. For most of the
past half century I've been listening to the endless (and pointless) conversation around casino poker rooms about which starting hand is favored over which other starting hand, interspersed
with equally pointless after-the-fact calculation of what odds a player
defeated in drawing out to win a pot, and on and on and on ad
nauseum—and while there's nothing in the record to indicate that
John Nash was a poker player, I am dead certain that in his jour-
neys along Nuthouse Row he met a lot of odds-calculating Hold
'Em wizards who'd overfigured themselves into blithering idiots.

But relax, already. We're not going all John Nash in this chapter, because (1) in spite of evidence to the contrary, I'm really
not trying to drive you crazy by writing this book, and (2) we
don't have to emulate Nash because odds in Texas Hold 'Em are
so basic and easy to calculate that men with limited—and in some
cases, nonexistent—formal educations have figured them out. Johnny
Moss, for example, arguably the smartest poker player who ever
lived, barely finished fourth grade. The most common error made
in evaluating odds in Texas Hold 'Em is the failure to recognize
which calculations are relevant to skillful play and which calculations are merely Nash-like equations written across the window
and likely to drive you insane. In this chapter we're going to learn
the difference.

Many stud and draw players who take up Hold 'Em try to
use the same odds that they've mastered in those other games
and end up scratching their heads because their calculations never
seem to work out the way they're supposed to. Before we do
anything else, it's necessary to learn the difference in probabilities between Hold 'Em and other forms of poker such as draw
and stud, and why these differences exist.

Poker has always been a game of probabilities, in all likelihood dreamed up by traveling math-hip gypsies out to fleece the small-village hicks they'd run into while drifting from town to town. There's less likelihood of having a straight flush than any other hand, and that's why a straight flush beats all other combinations of cards. Math whizzes calculate the odds of being dealt a particular hand in draw or stud by dividing the number of five-card combinations that produce that hand by the total number of possible five-card combinations in a deck of fifty-two, and these same whizzes calculated eons ago that a pair exists in about 40 percent of the total possible five-card hands if dealt randomly clockwise around the table, as happens in normal poker games. And if you use draw or stud probabilities in figuring the odds in Texas Hold 'Em, your calculations will be wrong *every single time*.

As opposed to the 40 percent likelihood in draw or stud games, in Texas Hold 'Em the odds of a pair occurring in the five cards dealt faceup on the board are just about *60 percent* Why? Well actually there are *two* reasons for the difference: (1) the order of the deal and (2) community cards.

Hey, wake up! Pay attention here. The following few paragraphs contain the most technical data I'm going to give you, and believe me, I hate giving it as much as you hate receiving it, but understanding this crap is more important than anything else you're going to learn about playing the game. You may have to go over these paragraphs several times before you get it, but if you want to be a good Hold 'Em player you've simply got to make the effort. Golfers love walloping golf balls out of sight but hate chipping and putting drills, even though the best chippers and putters become the best players. Think of the following paragraphs as chipping and putting practice.

I said a moment ago that a pair occurs in about 40 percent of the possible five-card combinations in a deck of fifty-two, assuming that the cards are dealt clockwise around the table to the players, one at a time, as happens in five-card draw or five-card stud. That's still true, always has been and always will be. In order for the player to have a pair dealt to him in stud or draw, two things have to happen: (1) At least two cards of the same value must be in the portion of the deck dealt out to form the opening hands (instead of the situation where one card is in the portion dealt and the other three of the same value are in the bottom third of the deck among the undealt cards), and (2) both of these cards must be dealt to the same player. But for a pair to appear when five cards are dealt off the top of the deck *in sequence*, as happens in Hold 'Em, both cards forming the pair need only be among the cards dealt, because the cards on the board are *common to all players in the hand*. By eliminating the necessity for both cards to be dealt to a certain player, the odds in Hold 'Em are made drastically different from the odds in any other form of poker.

What follows is the right way to figure the odds of a pair appearing on the board in Texas Hold 'Em. I recommend that you get out a deck of cards and follow along as I lead you through the process.

First shuffle and cut. Then turn the top card faceup, and for example's sake, let's call that card the 4 of clubs. Lay the 4 on the table. Then slide the second card slightly clear of the rest of the deck, hold it between your thumb and forefinger, and prepare to turn the second card faceup alongside the first.

Hold it. . . . Think for a few seconds about what's going to happen here.

You've seen one card in the deck, the 4 of clubs, and you're about to deal four more cards faceup beside it. So how many cards are left in the deck that will create a pair if matched up with the 4 of clubs?

If you said three, you've hit the nail on the head. There are three 4s left in the deck, a spade, a heart, and a diamond, and those are the cards that, if dealt, will create a pair on the board.

There is one more thing you must know in order to compute the odds of another four appearing, and that is the total number of cards left in the deck that you haven't seen. Well, you've only seen one card, so the answer is obviously fifty-one. So what are the chances of the next card, the one you still hold facedown by its corner, being a 4?

Easy, you say. Three in fifty-one, or 3/51 if expressed as a fraction.

Right on. If you know the number of cards left in the deck that will successfully make your hand, and also know the total number of cards that you haven't seen, then determining your chances of making your hand is as easy as falling off a log.

I think the proper formula's better expressed in the Little Black Book currently inside the Poker Pigeon's safe-deposit box, hidden from the public at large: **The odds of any one upcard yet to be dealt on the board being just the card needed to fill out any hand are** *the number of cards left in the deck that help the hand, divided by the total number of cards that the player hasn't seen.*

And if you're one of the sharpies in the audience, please refrain from snickering or going, "Well, *duh*-uh." The other students have to learn this just as you once did. Be as courteous as a Boy Scout. Your mother may be watching from above.

And if you're not one of the sharpies, please note that we're not quite finished here, so don't turn the second card faceup until we are. Now we're ready to fall off the log. See how easy it is?

Before you flip the next card faceup, let's carry the formula one step further. We've already determined that the odds of the *next* upcard being a 4 are three in fifty-one. So considering the knowledge that there are four more cards still to be dealt until there is a total of five on the board, please tell the class the correct odds of *any one* of the cards left to be dealt being a 4. Go up to the blackboard and show us your calculations.

What's that? You don't know the answer? Is that why you're standing there like a statue as you clutch the chalk in a death grip?

I hate for you to be embarrassed in front of the class, so . . . listen, I wouldn't do this for just anybody, but since you're the teacher's pet around here I'm going to let you cheat a little bit. Not one word to the rest of the class about me going to my safe-deposit box and providing you with *(bugle sounds and drumroll)* . . .

The Poker Pigeon's Black Book Item #2: **The odds, in Texas Hold 'Em, of *any one* of the cards remaining to be dealt improving any hand, are** *the number of cards left in the deck that improve the hand, times the number of cards left to be dealt, divided by the number of cards in the deck that the player hasn't seen.*

Huh? What did you say?

Relax, it isn't as hard as it sounds. As in most things mathematical, an example follows that will be clearer than the instruction itself. Just follow these easy steps.

The only card you've seen thus far is a 4. There are three more 4s in the deck, *and*: The number of cards yet to be dealt out on the board is *four*.

Hence, the number of cards left in the deck that pair the 4 you've seen is *three*, and the number of cards left to be dealt is *four*. So, in accordance with Black Book Item #2, you must multiply three times *four*. $3 \times 4 = 12$.

The number of unseen cards in the deck is still 51. *Therefore*: The odds of any one of the remaining cards to be dealt being a 4 are twelve in fifty-one, or between a 23 percent and 24 percent chance that we're going to see another 4 on the board.

(Note that I didn't say *exactly* 23 percent or *exactly* 24 per-cent. John Nash—and quite a few veteran Hold 'Em players who've blown their stacks just as Nash did—would disagree. John Nash would insist on computing the precise figure, which is 23.529 percent—rounded to the nearest thousandth of a percent, if that sort of thing matters to you—and he'd also insist that I'm wrong by telling you different, because math is the only exact science left to man. But then I'm not the one who's spent a good por-tion of his life sitting around in a straitjacket, am I? You simply don't have the time to compute the exact percentages in your head while playing poker—or if you do, I'm going to lock you in the interview room and call for the same herd of shrinks who spent decades studying Nash—so the figure we're looking for is one that's merely close enough for government work. If you know that the percentages of helping your hand in the next four cards is between 23 percent and 24 percent, then you also know that the odds against a second 4 appearing on the board are slightly greater than three to one, and that's all the knowledge that you need.)

Now.

Turn the next card off of the deck faceup, and place it gen-tly next to the 4 of clubs.

Aha. In this imaginary scenario, we have now plucked the jack of hearts from the deck. So what are the odds of a second *jack* appearing among the cards remaining to be dealt? Do your own work, now. Don't peek ahead.

You finished?

Okay, there are three more jacks in the deck, and three more cards to be dealt, and now that we've seen another card there are only fifty left that we haven't seen. So our odds of pairing the jack are $3 \times 3/50$, or $9/50$.

Is that the figure that you arrived at? Great, if you did. If you didn't, go back and reread Black Book Item #2, and recompute your figures until you get them right.

And finally, using the same formula, compute the chances of pairing the third card you're about to deal off of the deck, and then the fourth card, assuming that the board hasn't paired by the time you get to those. Take your time, this isn't any speed-reading course.

You got it?

Right. The chances of pairing the third card are $3 \times 2/49$, or $6/49$, and the chances of pairing the fourth card are $3 \times 1/48$, or $3/48$.

That wasn't so hard, was it? Now for our final exercise, we are going to compute the total chances of a pair appearing among five cards dealt in sequence from the top of the deck. This is what old John Nash would call an arithmetic progression, kids, and it works like this: **The chances of a pair appearing among five sequential cards are equal to the sum of the chances of pairing each individual card.**

So now we gotta add $12/51$(odds on pairing the first card) + $9/50$(odds on pairing the second card) + $6/49$(odds on pairing the third card) + $3/48$(odds on pairing the fourth card). $12/51 + 9/50 + 6/49 + 3/48 = x$.

Now, to properly compute the exact chance of pairing any one of four sequential cards, you must first determine the least common denominator between 51, 50, 49 and 48, and then you must divide the least common denominator by—

John Nash, shut your mouth! *I'm* **teaching this shit, so go back to your seat on the funny farm.**

I don't have the slightest idea what the least common denominator between 51, 50, 49, and 48 might be, and since I'm going to be computing odds in the middle of a poker game, I won't have the time to figure out exactly what that common denominator is. But all four numbers are awfully close to 50, aren't they? So in adding the four fractions let's pretend that they are all expressed in 50ths. We'll now add the following: approximately

12/50 + approximately 9/50 + approximately 6/50 + approximately 3/50.

Our total is approximately 30/50, and that means that a pair will appear among five sequential cards *just about 60 percent of the time*. And remember that we're using "approximately" and "just about" here. If we'd gone with old Nashie's method, we would have eventually come up with the *exact* answer, but it wouldn't have been significantly different than what we've already got, and during the time it took us to find a common denominator the other players would have gotten really pissed, and we probably would have found ourselves on our asses outside the poker room. In figuring poker odds, you need only be close enough for government work. Remember that.

And if you have the time, I'll invite you to test me here. Take the deck you've been using to follow along, shuffle, deal seven five-card hands clockwise around the table, then look to see how many of those hands contain pairs or better. When you've finished that, shuffle once more, and this time, create seven hands by taking five cards *in sequence* from the top of the deck and pushing the hands off to one side each time you deal the fifth card, so that when you're finished you have seven separate poker hands laid out. Now look to see how many of the sequentially dealt hands contain pairs. You're going to be amazed at the difference between the hands dealt sequentially and the hands dealt clockwise. And if that doesn't satisfy you, try the preceding a *hundred* times. John Nash would say that a *million* such tests would barely begin to set the trend, but then old John has more free time than any of us, doesn't he? About 40 percent of the five hands dealt clockwise will contain pairs, while about 60 percent of the hands dealt sequentially will have pairs in them. The important thing for you to do is test the theory often enough to make you comfortable, and to never take anyone, including me, strictly at their word when it comes to poker odds.

And now you have all the knowledge that you need to compute the odds of any card combination appearing in Texas Hold 'Em. Yeah, you do. Stop shaking your head. It's like in grammar-school math where you learned long division. It would be impossible for a math book to list every number that might be divided into any other number, but if you learned the formula for long division you could work any problem containing numbers of every multiple of digits imaginable. Same with Hold 'Em. There might be any number of situations where you need to compute the odds of certain cards falling off the deck, and if you learn the formulas I just gave you, you can very quickly do so.

With the odds of the board pairing out of the way, here we go with Black Book Item #3, as follows: **The only odds of any consequence in Texas Hold 'Em are the chances of improving a hand consisting of the two pocket cards that the player holds, combined with the three cards on the board once the flop is dealt. All other statistics are irrelevant, including the pre-flop odds of one two-card hand beating another two-card hand, and what odds some dumb sonofabitch overcame in drawing out on some poker hustler's hand a half-hour ago.**

And Black Book Item #4: **In order to win consistently at limit Texas Hold 'Em, you must either hold the best hand after the flop and have it stand up, or, if you don't have the best hand, you must know the odds of improving your hand once you've seen the flop, and only when the payoff for winning the hand is greater than the odds against it do you continue to draw. All else you'll hear about the game is bullshit.**

Right now you're probably thinking, your eyes narrowing in suspicion, *Wait a minute. If all that's true, how come you just spent ten pages talking about the odds of a pair appearing on the board? The board pairing's got nothing to do with making draws. You trying to waste our time or something?*

Not at all, even though you're right to think that the odds of the board pairing have nothing to do with the actual playing of a hand. The odds of pairing the board, however, are the best and simplest method of explaining the computation of odds that *do* matter.

You remember a few chapters ago where I said that a tightass can't possibly win in Texas Hold 'Em? The tightass sits in a game for hours waiting for premium starting cards and only plays in pots where he thinks his hand is the best before the flop. And he's right, in that where you have the best hand, you're supposed to bet it strongly—but it's also true that the best hand before the flop stands up to win in limit Hold 'Em far less than half the time. Furthermore, since everyone in the game already has the tightass's style of play figured out, the other players will fold when the tightass bets and he'll profit very little from the pots that he wins. To win pots of any size, you must do some drawing out of your own and make a few straights and flushes, though you must not chase hands where the odds against you winning are greater than the payoff you'll receive.

So, using the same formula as we did in computing the odds of a pair coming on the board, figure the odds of making a flush where, after the flop, two suited cards are in your hand to go with two of the same suit now on the board. And after you do that, compute the odds of filling an open-ended straight draw.

First the flush: If you have four spades after the flop, there are nine more spades that fill your hand left in the deck. Also there are two more cards to be dealt, and since you've seen five cards up to this point (your pocket cards and the three flop cards), there are forty-seven cards in the deck that you haven't seen. The number of remaining spades (9) times the number of cards to be dealt (2), divided by the number of unseen cards (47) gives the fraction 18/47, meaning that the odds of you making your flush are eighteen in forty-seven, better expressed as odds of 29 to 18 *against* you making your flush, just slightly worse than three to two. With that knowledge, you now know that you should never draw for a flush head-up against only one player. You draw for flushes where there are two or more others in the pot besides you, and the payoff you receive if you win is at least twice the amount you're risking. (And by the way, if you're an old draw or stud player, you also know that the odds of making a one-card draw to a flush in either of those games are about *one in five,* and that's why you'll see flushes and straights many times more often in Hold 'Em than in the games you cut your teeth on.)

If you have an open-ended straight draw after the flop, the chances of making your hand (using the same formula as in the preceding paragraph) are 16 in 47, better expressed as 31 to 16, or much closer to two to one than the odds of making a flush.

(And here, we'll point out another oddity peculiar to Texas Hold 'Em—and something that Analytical Man will surely include during his I'm-smart monologue—that the odds of making a flush in Hold 'Em are greater than the odds of making a straight, and therefore in Hold 'Em a straight should actually *beat* a flush, even though that isn't the case because the hand rankings in Hold 'Em remain the same as in other poker games. That the percentages of having a flush are greater than those of having a straight is useless information unless you're drawing for one of those hands and realize that there should be about 15 percent more money in the pot to justify drawing for a straight than to justify drawing for a flush. Also—and this is just common sense talking—you should never draw for a straight when three cards of the same suit appear on the flop. With three-of-a-suit on the board, it's a dead cinch that at least one of your opponents has a card of the same suit so that not only are your opponents' odds of making a flush greater than your own odds of making a straight, but two cards—the ones of the same suit as the cards on the board that will also fill your straight—are now eliminated from your own list of wins, and your chances of making your straight and winning the pot are reduced from 16 in 47 to 12 in 47.)

Straight-making odds and flush-making odds will cover ninety percent of the to-draw-or-not-to-draw choices open to you, so if you memorize the chances of making these hands, ninety percent of all your at-the-table calculation needs will be covered. Here's a good rule of thumb: If you're drawing for a flush there should be two players in the pot, and when you're drawing for a straight you should be up against 3 opponents. Even though in actuality it's okay to take a flyer on a straight if there's 15 percent more in the pot than the amount needed to justify a flush draw, you'll be a real pain in the ass to the other players if you hold up the game to count the pot (not to mention that everyone in the room will know that you're on a draw), so in the long run you'll be better off by just refusing to draw for a straight unless the game at that point is at least four-handed.

Here I should mention another useless tidbit that you'll hear around most poker parlors, another taste of pseudo-wisdom that you'll be better off to ignore. Rest assured that the Hold 'Em-playing John Nashes that you'll run across, doomsayers to the very end, will gladly point out that even if you make your flush, unless you hold the ace of the needed suit, you might lose to a higher flush. That's true; that downside happens occasionally. It's also true that it rains occasionally in Texas in August, but that doesn't mean you should put on a slicker and galoshes every time you go outside. You don't know anyone else's hand, so if you're drawing for a flush, you've got to assume that your hand will win if you make it and play accordingly. If you do make a flush and someone beats you anyway, that's just Hold 'Em's version of tough shit. The major mistake that weaker players make in such situations is that, when they're drawing for a spade flush and old Spadey hits the board on Fifth Street, the bona fide pigeon always raises any bet made. If you hold the 9-10 of spades in your hand, you make a flush on the end, and Chip-Shuffling Man bets right on into you—*that's* the time you should only call.

You'll also hear, usually from Analytical Man, what the odds are of making these hands with only *one* card left to be dealt. There are certain times when knowing your odds with only one card to come really matters, but they are few and far between. Analytical Man's talking primarily about someone's chances of making their hand when they have nothing after the flop and then *pick up* a draw on the turn, but if you don't have what you believe is the best hand, or at the very least a one-card *draw* to a winning hand when the flop hits the deck, you should never stick around to see Fourth Street. Once again: When you hear these meaningless odds spouted forth, you must ignore Analytical Man and his bullshit, and keep your eye firmly on the prize. (The only instance I can think of where the odds with one to come are important occurs when you have flopped a big hand, either a set or two pair, and after the turn card appears it becomes obvious through betting patterns that someone has hit a flush or straight. If you have a set with one card to come and someone else has made a straight or flush, your chances of making quads or a full house and drawing *back* out are 10 in 46, and, if you hold two pair instead of a set, your odds of filling up are 6 in 46. At that point you should examine the pot odds you're receiving and make the decision on whether to call or fold accordingly. Nearly everyone else in the game, including the poker hustlers, will make the mistake of seeing the river card in this situation, regardless of the odds, and making proper decisions here will give you a leg up on the field.)

In line with the sage advice of the preceding paragraph, let's examine the figures that shoot holes in any analysis of odds other than the ones existent after the flop. Even *good* Hold 'Em players' most common mistake is to draw when they shouldn't, and this error usually occurs when five to seven players call multiple raises to see the flop. If you watch enough of these hands, you'll understand just how much of an advantage you create for yourself by not sticking around until Fourth Street when you don't have the best hand after the flop or when the flop doesn't produce a draw for you.

Say you've got the button and come into a triple-raised pot with 89 of hearts and there are six players in the hand opposing you. Say the flop is the K of spades, the 3 of diamonds, and the 2 of hearts, giving you no hand whatsoever. You do have remote flush possibilities if two consecutive hearts happen to hit the board, and you'll probably also win the pot if you catch two running 8s, two running 9s, or an 8 *and* a 9 (and pigs may sprout wings, and someday the Texas Rangers might win the American League). If you could be a fly on the wall listening to the casino coffee shop's dinner conversation (and this is another excellent reason not to associate with any of the players away from the game: they'll give you really crappy ideas), some so-called poker hustler would say something like, "Man, if that pot gets big enough you gotta draw no matter what, even if all you got is a draw *to* a draw." The urge to fit this poker hustler for a dunce cap would be strong, but you'd be better off resisting even though this hustler is in reality a dyed-in-the-wool sucker. What follows are the actual odds of making any draw when you must hit two consecutive cards.

You read a few pages back that your chances of hitting a draw where you only need one card to fill your hand are the number of cards left in the deck that help you, times the number of cards left to be dealt, divided by the total number of cards in the deck that you haven't seen, and that the odds of making a flush where you have four-of-a-suit after the flop are 18 in 47. Well and good. But here you're going to learn how to compute the odds of hitting any *two consecutive* cards to make a hand using the Poker Pigeon's Black Book Item #5, as follows: **The odds, in Texas Hold 'Em of catching two consecutive cards to make a hand are the odds of hitting the first helping card times the odds of hitting the second helping card.** Here John Nash would roll up his sleeves, grab a magic marker, and haul ass over to his dormitory window.

If you hold the 89 of hearts and there is one heart (the deuce) on the board, that means that there are ten hearts left in the deck, and there are forty-seven total cards left that you haven't seen. 10×2 (2 being the number of cards left to be dealt)/47, or 20/47, then, are the odds of one of the two remaining cards to be dealt being a heart. Then, if you are fortunate enough to catch a heart on the turn, your odds of catching *another* heart on the river become 9 (the remaining hearts in the deck) $\times$ 1(only one left to be dealt)/46 (the number of cards in the deck you haven't seen), or 9/46. 9/46 (the odds of catching the second heart) $\times$ 10/47 (the odds of catching the first heart) = 90/2162, or just a hair greater than a 4 percent chance of hitting two consecutive hearts to make a flush. In your other winning two-card possibility (two consecutive 8s, two running 8s, or an 8 *and* a 9), there are six helping cards of which you must catch two in a row to make a hand. Using the same formula as we did in figuring the odds of making a flush, you will find that the odds of hitting two 8s, two 9s, or an 8 *and* a 9, are a tiny bit less than 3 percent, and, added to the 4 percent chance of making a flush make your total odds of winning the pot about 7 percent. In other words, the odds of you making a hand are just about one in fourteen, and in this scenario there are six players in the pot besides you, so your payoff if you make the flush or catch the needed combination of 8s and/or 9s, is six to one.

Q. What should you do, class?

A. THROW THE SONOFABITCH AWAY.

As a matter of fact, since only ten players can sit in a Hold 'Em game, the best pot odds you can hope for are nine to one—and you get those odds only when *no one* folds before the flop. It's more than sufficient to say that you should *never* continue to draw after the flop if you need two consecutive cards to win. This is always true and will remain true no matter how long you sit in a game and watch player after player raking in pots after drawing two cards out of their ass. In the long run, if you never continue to draw when you need two cards to win, you'll be far and away ahead of the game.

Here I should mention another urban legend told among the poker hustlers, that if the pot gets big enough, you should even draw for a "middle-buster" (an old-time poker term for an inside straight). Actually, the myth about drawing for the inside straight is better advice than the one about drawing when you need two consecutive cards to fill your hand—but not much. Where you need one card to fill a straight, there are four cards in the deck that make your hand, and after the flop your odds of making the straight are 8 in 47, or just about one in six. So it's okay to draw for an inside straight where the pot is laying you seven to one, though the times in limit poker where seven players will see the flop in a ten-handed game are few and far between.

We're almost through with the math lesson, but I think we

need one more example to really bolster the advice given in the preceding couple of paragraphs. Remember the chapter on playing weak hands well, where I said that the chances of hitting two cards on the flop to help 10,4 are slightly less than one in thirteen? We come up with those odds this way: There are six cards (three more 10s and three more 4s) in the deck that help this hand, and our odds of flopping the first helping card are 18/50. After we catch the first helping card, that leaves five more helping cards in the deck that must fall among the other two that make up the flop, so the odds against hitting the second helping card become 10/59. By multiplying these two fractions we get 180/2450, which reduces to 18/245, or the odds of just less than one in thirteen that are expressed above.

"Jesus Christ," you say, "not *another* fraction!"

Well, yeah, but this is nearly the last one, and it connects with a very strong point I'm trying to make. The mathematical odds of catching two cards on the flop to help 10-4 are one in thirteen. The odds of making a winning hand when you must catch consecutive cards on the turn and on the river are one in fourteen. If you see the flop with 10-4 and catch nothing to help you, you can quickly dispose of the hand and be out only the pre-flop money. But if you continue to draw where you need two cards to win you're also going to fork over the after-the-flop tariff and, should you catch one of your cards on the turn, forfeit the larger bets you'll have to see to look at the river card.

Considering the above information, which would you say is the dumber play: coming into a pot in early position with 10-4 or continuing to draw after the flop when you need two consecutive cards in order to win? In view of the odds against and potential risk for each, the answer is obvious, and all those poker hustlers who claim that there are times when you should see the river no matter what the flop produces are full of it up to here.

Before we move on to greener pastures, we have to discuss

one more situation, that being the occasional hand where you are actually the favorite to win when you're on a draw—and at the same time we'll shoot holes in the myths about "overcards" (two pocket cards that are larger than anything on the board, even though you've failed to make a pair on the flop). You'll learn by listening to the experts that when you have both a straight draw *and* a flush draw after the flop, you're the favorite in the hand even though you don't have the winner at that point. Well, figures.don't lie, and here the experts are right without any question. When you have nine cards left to make a flush and six non-flush cards in the deck that make you a straight, that totals up to fifteen wins, or odds of 30 in 47 of making either a straight or flush and winning the money. In that situation you should raise the maximum possible after the flop and see the hand through to the end, even though you have only a draw at that point.

Where I differ from most experts is when you have a flush draw to go with a couple of overcards. Say you have AK of hearts and the flop produces the 4 and 5 of hearts, and the 9 of spades. Here, many so-called pros would give you the same chance of winning as when you have a straight and a flush draw, because the six cards left in the deck that pair your overcards added to the nine cards that fill in your flush total fifteen potential wins, the same as when you have both straight and flush possibilities. I think the experts' reasoning here is all wet. You should *never* count cards that could pair your overcards as potential wins because too often a card that pairs your ace or king will also produce *two* pair for one of your opponents. It's somewhat of an oddity in Hold 'Em that many very good players will draw when they only have overcards to play with, counting the six remaining cards that pair one of their pocket cards as wins, and will completely dismiss the idea that even if they pair one of their overcards, they're very likely to lose the pot anyway. I won't draw at overcards and, when I have a flush draw consisting of two-of-a-suit on the board to go with two-of-a-suit in my hand, both of my pocket cards also being overcards, I count only my possible flush as a win and play this hand the same as any other flush draw. I believe with all my heart that this is the correct winning strategy and that those who count the potential of pairing overcards as wins will come out on the short end of the stick in the long run. I have no statistics to back me up here, only a belief that drawing at overcards is terribly poor strategy. Once again, however, just as with all my opinions where I have no numbers to back me up, the way that you want to play 'em is up to you.

So we're about finished here, and right now, before you ever take another seat in a Hold 'Em game, you know a few tricks that very few poker hustlers understand. It will be much to your advantage to never give these secrets away. The beauty of what you've learned in this chapter is that all of your odds calculations are done in your head, and when you toss your hands away no one in the game is going to see your cards. You should never even *pretend* to know anything about odds. Desperate Man and his friends will think nothing of you throwing hands away, and all that they'll remember about you will be the time you won a pot in early position with 10-4. If you're smart, you'll never waver from the image you're creating and will do nothing whatsoever to change those poker sharks' minds.

Is your attention span about at its limits? Well, I'm not surprised, and I think it's time to wrap this chapter up. We could probably go on for another thousand pages, giving example after example of the odds of doing this or that and how to compute them in various situations, but every example would come back to the simple formulas expressed in these pages. If you memorize the formulas and practice using them in actual play, in a very short time you'll be able to figure odds on the run as well as any pro. Furthermore, you'll have a serious advantage in that since you're the pigeon, no one else at the table will think you're smart enough to compute mathematical probability. In the instances where you fold your hand based on your odds calculations, you'll *never* show your cards to anyone or discuss why you're making these plays, and just because you fold occasionally the hustlers won't give your play any more credit than they already have. Once again, that's the real lesson this book is trying to put across: as long as you continue to make the right play while sitting there looking dumb, you can go on picking the hustlers' pockets while never exposing the strength of your game.

8

Location, Location, Location

Years ago I played some poker with a guy named Harry "Half-a-Point" Brown, who cooked a mean cheeseburger and made mouthwatering fresh-cut french fries. Because of his kitchen skills Half-a-Point had chow hall duty during his six months in the federal pen for bookmaking, and since the cooks all lived in one-man cells in the joint, his culinary skills might've also saved him from spending some facedown time with his nose pressed against the mattress after the lights went out. Or so Half used to tell it. You'd just have to know the guy.

Once back out on the street, Half decided he needed a legitimate front to make his parole officer quit bugging him, so he leased a short-order restaurant in the Polytechnic section of Fort Worth. The closed-down greasy spoon was near Texas Wesleyan University on Vaughn Boulevard, a once busy thoroughfare that had fallen on hard times since a six-lane freeway had routed the majority of the traffic elsewhere. Once upon a time the place had been standing room only, and Half thought he could restore the restaurant's former glory in no time flat, but try as he might and however he adjusted his menu, Half-a-Point Brown couldn't seem to attract the customers.

The consensus was that Half was fast going broke in the restaurant business and, since he never saw two pocket cards that he didn't envision as the nuts, there was a noticeable sagging of shoulders and hanging of heads around the poker table whenever players speculated on his chances of ever playing in the game again. Then one day, Half brightened moods considerably by showing up for the game driving a Lincoln and exhibiting a pocket full of cash, and dropping a couple thousand bucks in just a few hours' play. On that day, he told the guys that he'd finally hit on the right restaurant formula, and we were all happy for him— not to mention happy for ourselves because the game was about to get really good. A few days later, I drove by the restaurant and it didn't seem to have any more customers than before. Shortly thereafter, Half-a-Point's parole officer had him picked up on a violation, the P.O.'s charge being that Half had returned to taking football bets. Half-a-Point Brown swore to his dying day—when he suffered a heart attack while making book over the phone— that his parole officer had framed him, but you know what? I don't think I ever really believed the guy; I also thought that poor location had done in the restaurant along with Half-a-Point Brown's only-ever attempt at legitimacy.

Another regular in the poker game was a guy who owned an Italian restaurant with a worse location in Dallas than Half-a-Point's failed venture ever thought about having. The Italian place was hidden on a has-been street in a dilapidated has-been business neighborhood, had cramped and limited slant-in parking out front, and was just a two-minute drive from an Olive Garden that was nestled beside a freeway in an upscale modern shopping center. Yet even with the lousy location and nearby competition, the Italian place always had a line out front waiting for seating, and the guy who owned it was making a fortune.

"Jesus Christ," you say, "what's all this got to do with playing poker?"

I'm getting to that.

The Italian restaurant had stood in the same place for around forty years, the current owner's father and uncle having started the business just after WWII, when the neighborhood was booming, businesswise. Over the years the eatery developed a reputation for serving the best pizza, pasta dishes, and scrumptious crab claw appetizers south of Philadelphia—plus it didn't hurt that most of the square-john customers thought that the original owners had Mafia ties since there's nothing more exciting to the average working stiff than sitting in a darkened booth eating ravioli while speculating whether the handsome olive-complexioned guy at the bar might be a hit man. So well managed and well reputed was the Italian restaurant that its location didn't hamper its success.

Shortly after Half-a-Point Brown's short-order joint closed down, I ran into the guy who owned the Italian place and asked him straight-out why he thought his own restaurant was so successful while Half's place had failed so miserably. He tilted his head in thought, scratched his scalp through thinning hair, then told me, "Well, I don't pay location all that much never-mind. We're serving serious food and know how to please the customer, and if you do that, the customer's gonna seek you out even if you're on the fuckin' moon. But where you're servin' hamburgers, hell, you see one hamburger you seen 'em all. People that eat hamburger all the time got no taste to begin with and just want to eat on the run, so if you're sellin' hamburger, you gotta be located where they can see your sign and get in and out in a hurry. They're sellin' B, we're sellin' A. If your food's good enough and you know your business, you can make money anywhere."

So before you start snoring on me, here's how these two stories relate to the upcoming poker lesson. Neither Half nor the

Italian restaurant guy respected business location, and both were lousy position players in the Texas Hold 'Em game, but there was a major difference. Not only was Half-a-Point Brown a business failure but he lost a lot more money playing poker than his bookmaking operation ever profited, and when he died, the poker players had to take up a collection to pay for burying the guy. Conversely, not only did the Italian restaurant guy make a fortune from his business but he also beat some of the toughest poker games in the country to death over a twenty-year period, and even though he's now in his eighties and doesn't get to play all that much, when he does show up for a game he always holds his own and then some. The guy has been a longtime puzzle to the Las Vegas crowd, most of whom think he should be losing his ass, just like Harry Brown always did, because the so-called pros think that position play is an important part—and, to hear many tell it, *the* most important part—of the game.

So who's right and who's wrong?

It's impossible to give a yes-or-no answer to that question. It's an answer *of sorts* to say that playing position isn't near as important as *knowing* position, but since that statement is likely to twist your brain into knots, I gotta figure out a better method of getting my point across. To put it simply, if you ignore position play the same way Half-a-Point Brown ignored position play, you've got no chance to win, but if you ignore position in the same way that the Italian restaurant guy ignored position, you could well dominate any game that you play in. And with that said, I'll now launch into a few anecdotes/examples. Teaching by example might be the long way around the block, but it's still the best way. And you in the back row there, quit snickering and elbowing your buddy, or leave.

Before I met the Italian restaurant guy, I was just like most young Hold 'Em players, listening closely to the so-called pros and doing everything in my power to play exactly like they did.

In the small-blind position I tossed my hand in without looking at it, and in the big-blind position I wouldn't call a raise without AA, KK, or AK—and if there were a couple of pre-flop raises, even AK went into the discards. The closer I sat to the button the weaker the hand I'd come in with, and . . . well, I think you get the picture. I did all of that good professional stuff, you know? I was twenty-five years old the first time I saw the Italian restaurant guy annihilate a game, and it was through watching him that I began to change my mind about the best way to play position.

For the purposes of this discussion let's call the Italian restaurant guy "Big Al," because "Italian restaurant guy" becomes a real tongue-twister if you repeat it often enough. He wasn't really big and his name wasn't really Al, but since his reputation as having ties to the Mafia kept people scared to death of him, Big Al is better than most pseudonyms you could use. He had thin black hair, wide beefy shoulders, and wore lots of gold chains around his neck and diamonds on his fingers. For some reason he took a liking to me.

Watching Big Al was a major eye-opener. He ignored nearly everything I'd learned about position play, and since the pros considered playing position the be-all and end-all, I probably would have marked Big Al down as just another weak player if it he hadn't won both consistently and big. And he wasn't up against a bunch of pushovers, either; the game in question was held daily at the American Veterans of Foreign Wars' Club on Dallas's Lower Greenville Avenue and, during the 1960s, '70s and early '80s, was one of the toughest poker games to be found anywhere in the world. Not only were the regulars in the Amvets' game plenty legendary on their own—Bob Hooks, Cowboy Wolford, Troy Phillips (a professional-quality player who was most famous for being shot in the gonads by his ex-wife, Candy Barr, the stripper who later moved to Los Angeles and became Mickey Cohen's girlfriend for a time), Charles Harrelson (right, *that*

Charles Harrelson—Woody Harrelson's father who's currently serving life in the pen for murdering a federal judge), and the not-related-to-each-other Smith boys (1981 Main Event finalist Ken and 1985 World Series Main Event champion Bill), to name a few—but every well-known road gambler who passed through town had to drop in and give the Amvets' game a try. Brunson was an occasional visitor, as were Bobby Baldwin, Hal Fowler, Amarillo Slim Preston, Stu Ungar, etc., etc., etc., all either in, or major candidates for, the Poker Hall of Fame. Big Al played with them all, and in the long run came out far, far ahead.

The most enlightening afternoon I ever spent during my early poker career happened one summer day during the early 1970s, when I showed up for the limit game at the Amvets' too late to get a seat. The game generally kicked off around noon. I came at one o'clock to find the ten-and-twenty Hold 'Em ten-handed, with five or six names already on the waiting list. I added my name to the list and sat down at a nearby empty poker table. I wasn't exactly filled with hope; normally when the game was full, if a seat didn't open up by three o'clock, there wasn't going to *be* a seat for the rest of that day, so I planned to wait until three, then leave if I wasn't in action. As it turned out I was still rooted to my seat when the game broke up around midnight, even though I hadn't played a hand.

The club was on the top floor of a pre-WWII-vintage two-story building, with a bar in the lobby and a kitchen in back, and four or five poker tables set up in one giant room with faded, dusty carpet on the floor. Nearly everyone smoked while playing poker back in those days. The only sounds were the muted conversation from the poker table, the humming of a window a/c unit, and the chug of a smoke-dissipating exhaust fan. As I flopped down in my chair, Big Al sat directly across the table from me, waiting for a seat just as I was. His name was above mine on the waiting list.

Most serious poker players, when they aren't actually playing the game, spend a lot of time watching poker, talking about poker, or reading about poker, so much so that poker has gone beyond being a profitable pastime or profession and has become an obsessive-compulsive disorder. I don't think that the Poker 24/7 Syndrome is healthy, and in later years I've done my best to forget about poker unless I'm playing, but in those days I was just as guilty of dwelling on poker as the next obsessive-compulsive guy. From the second I sat down on that day at the Amvets', I was as absorbed in the ten-and-twenty limit game going on twenty feet away as if I was playing in it myself. I watched every player's every move like a hawk, sometimes rising partway out of my chair to see the cards on the board, in my own mind deciding in advance what each player's move should be and, after the hand was over, critiquing the player's actions if they were different than what I would have done.

It was around mid-afternoon when I saw the most important poker hand—at least where development of my own game is concerned—that I ever witnessed, and the hand is burned into my consciousness as if it happened yesterday instead of over thirty years ago in a game where I wasn't even a player. There were no famous poker players involved and there weren't any giant piles of cash on the line; the poker hand that turned my life around happened in a ten-and-twenty game with a hundred-or-so bucks in the pot. Three or four players had seen the flop and, after the post-flop bets and raises, the hand came down to head-up action between a guy called Inky and a guy called Pig. (Really, that's what everyone called the two guys.) Inky had the seat to the left of the big blind and Pig was on the button. Inky had raised before the flop and Pig had only called. The flop produced K♥, Q♣,4♦. Inky bet in first position and, after the other players had all tossed in their cards, Pig raised. Inky re-raised and Pig raised a second time as well. Inky called and the hand moved on to Fourth Street.

And, closeby on my left, Big Al half-whispered, "Ace-king and jack-ten."

I stared at him across the table. "Huh?" I said.

"Inky's holding ace-king and Pig's got jack-ten," Big Al said softly. "Want to bet? Nothing big, just to make it innerstin'." He popped a five-dollar bill onto the table.

I glanced down at the money, then back up at Big Al. "So when did you change your name to Kreskin?" I said.

"My money's up," Big Al said. "How about yours?"

I confidently pulled a five from the bankroll in my pocket and dropped the bill down next to Big Al's. Christ, *no one* could read players that well. I thought that this was going to be the easiest five bucks I'd ever made. I turned my attention back to the game, where Fourth Street had produced the six of diamonds.

Inky bet twenty dollars. This time, Pig merely called.

And the dealer showed Fifth Street, the ace of hearts.

Big Al murmured, "Now old Inky's *really* fucked."

"No way can you be sure of that," I said.

"You can double the bet if you wanta," Big Al said.

A warning bell went off in my brain. I shook my head.

Inky now bet again. Pig appeared to pause in thought, then raised. Inky looked in dejection at the board, then put twenty bucks more in chips in the pot to call. Pig showed his J10, giving him the nut straight. Inky rolled over his AK, uttered a cuss word, and then tossed his cards away in disgust. I thought that Inky was one helluva player (which he was and is) for not losing even more on the hand, because with the top two pair it was possible to have, I likely would have re-raised. Big Al chuckled, snatched up my five-dollar bill and stuck it in his pocket.

I felt a little shell-shocked as I got up and went around the table to sit down beside Big Al. "How the hell did you know what they had?" I said.

Big Al looked guardedly around to be sure that no one else was listening, then leaned closer and winked at me. "Easy. Inky's so tight he squeaks, and no way would he raise before the flop in early position without two aces, two kings, or ace-king. Pig's on the button and probably would have looked at the flop with just about any two cards, but when a king and a queen come on the flop, then in order to raise Inky's bet, Pig's gotta have jack-ten for an open-end straight draw. Think back, huh? If Pig had been holdin' two aces or two kings, or two *queens* even, he woulda double-raised before the flop. Pig knows Inky's a tightass and ain't gonna re-raise after the flop with top pair unless he's at least got a great big kicker. After Inky re-raises, Pig puts in another raise hopin' that if he doesn't make his straight on the turn, Inky's gonna check and then Pig can get himself a free draw on Fourth Street where the bet climbs up to twenty dollars. So really, knowin' Pig and knowin' his position play, it's pretty easy right there to put him on jack-ten.

"Up until Pig's re-raise after the flop," Big Al said, "Inky's hand was sort of a mystery. I mean, tight as he is, he's gotta have one of the top premium hands before he'd've raised before the flop sitting right beside the big blind, but I had no idea which of the big hands he really had. When Inky bet after that king hit the board on the flop, he might've had two aces or two kings— he woulda flopped a set with two pocket kings—or ace-king, which is the hand it turned out he *did* have. They're playin' a four-raise limit, and after Pig's re-raise there was still one raise left, and if Inky'd've had two aces or two kings in the pocket, he woulda capped the bets by raising again instead of just calling. Right there, when he smooth-called Pig's re-raise, I couldn't put him on any hand except ace-king. On Fourth Street, when the six come out on the board, Inky had to bet in self defense, because just in case Pig was on a draw—which it turned out that he was—Inky wouldn't be giving him a chance to check and get a free look at the last card. I think Pig coulda won the pot right there by raising on Fourth Street, and he woulda raised a lot of folks at that point, but no way was he going to raise a tightass like old Inky. Inky made a mistake by betting on Fifth Street when the ace hit the board, but I think making the top two pair sort of put him over the edge so that he acted on his hand without really studying the situation. You notice that after Pig raised on the end, Inky was through with raising, and I'll bet he thought hard about throwing his hand in right there instead of pissing off another twenty dollars by calling the guy. But that's how I knew what they had, the bets they made combined with the position they were in." Big Al finished speaking, leaned back and propped a knee against the edge of the table.

My mouth was open like a man's who's just watched a space ship land. I said to Big Al, "Look, all due respect, you're not known as an expert position player. So since you don't *play* position, how come you know so much about it?"

Big Al sort of shrugged. "What, you think I ain't played enough poker to figure out a few things?"

"You don't *play* position," I said again. "If you know that much about it, how come you don't play a better position game?"

Big Al scratched his chin in thought. "Son, I'm going to give you a lesson here. You don't think I play position, but most times I do. It's just that sometimes I stray from what's considered good position play to keep people from figuring out my hands. This is the difference between a fair poker player and a *good* poker player. A fair player learns a lotta rules and goes by 'em, and his play's okay because he's followin' those rules, but that's all it is, *only* okay, and he'll never be all that great of a player until he takes his game on up to the next level. A *good* player knows position and knows which players in the game are only *fair* players, meaning that they'll play position right down the line. If you know a guy's playing position and also know that he's only a fair player, then it's easy to figure out what he's got. And when you know how the other players play but they don't know how *you* play, then that's when you've got 'em by the gonads."

Out of the mouths of babes—or in this case, out of the mouths of tough-looking Italian guys . . . From that day forward I saw playing poker in an entirely different light, and I haven't seen anything over the past thirty years or so to change my mind. Almost to a man, self-imagined poker sharks play by certain rules and almost never deviate from them. If you can alter your own play so that the others don't know what you're doing, while you know by their actions exactly what your opponents are up to, then you're well on your way to becoming a consistent winner no matter what competition you're up against or whether you play position worth a damn.

So here we go with the Pigeon's #1 Postulate on Position Play. As I said earlier in this book, position play is of utmost importance before the flop, because there are certain hands that you *never* play in early position even though you should raise with identical hands where you're sitting on the button or in one of the two seats to the right of the button. That's Hold 'Em 101. But—and here's the rub to playing position—**Position play loses its importance after the flop, unless you're only a fair-to-mediocre player, because if you play at an advanced level, your actions in early position can offset or even be stronger than the mediocre player's actions in late position.**

And, yeah, that's a mouthful. So let's begin our discussion by talking about the self-imagined poker sharks' position play and how to spot certain moves to get a read on those players' hands in the same way that Big Al knew what Inky and Pig were holding. All position play is based on the rock-solid theory that **The later your position relative to the button, the more players'** actions you can observe before having to make your own playing decisions. Not only does having other players act before you give you an advantage in the overall playing of your hand but the decisions that you make in late position will be correct a much higher percentage of the time than the decisions you make in early position.

The above postulate is vintage Sklansky, and if you learn and practice this type of position play, you will have a big advantage in games stacked with novices and retards. The problem is this: Due to the nationwide Hold 'Em explosion, players are much more sophisticated overall than in the past, and those really soft games just don't exist anymore. So here's the Poker Pigeon's Second Postulate with regard to position: **There are competent position players in every game today, and to beat modern Hold 'Em consistently, not only must you understand others' position play well to properly put your opponents on certain pocket cards, you must also know how to alter your own play so as to destroy whatever advantage your opponents might have during the hand simply because of their position.**

Or as Johnny Moss once told me, "Them boys is fixin' to get better, so I gotta figure how to get better'n what they're fixin' to be."

So how do we go about gettin' better'n them when it comes to playing position? If you play with the same group day in and day out, it's pretty easy to learn the players' habits, but as a certified pigeon you're going to move a lot from game to game, a stupid expression on your face. As a newcomer to about every game you sit in, you must spend the first few times around the table playing your own cards strictly according to Sklansky and observing the talent around you. If you watch closely you'll have the competent players weeded out from the novices in no time at all by watching the two cards that players show down at the end. As we've harped on before, so-called experts won't play in the big or small blind positions without one of the three choicest hands, AA, KK, or AK. In what's called "middle position" (remember, I don't differentiate between early and middle positions, but most poker book authors define middle position as the fourth, fifth, and sixth seats to the left of the button in a ten-handed game), you should look for the hotshots to show down some AQs, KQs, AJs, A10s, and similar hands—even though I teach that playing any of these hands other than AQ is suicide unless you're in the 8th, 9th, or 10th (button) seat—along with suited connectors 78 and higher (so-called experts generally won't play 23, 34, 45, or 56 even if they're suited). You should concentrate only on the first seven seats in each hand in order to get a tell on individuals' play because even the self-imagined poker sharks are apt to come in with just about any two cards in late position—because that's what Sklansky told 'em to do, and by God, if Sklansky says it, that's the way it's gotta be. If you're observant and have a better-than-average memory, you should have the Sklansky disciples identified in pretty short order. The players who show down the weakest hands relative to their position will remain a mystery for the time being; they're either novices or Pigeons Who Would Be Winners like yourself, and you won't know which are which until you've seen some examples of their post-flop action. We'll talk about post-flop play shortly, but for now let's assume you've played four times around the table and have identified the sharks, and let's say that there are five of those guys with the rest of the field remaining mystery men.

You're on the button with KQ. One of the sharks sits to the left of the big blind, and this guy raises. Another shark calls the big blind *and* the raise from the sixth chair. So what do you do when it's your turn?

Simple. You fold.

"Wait a minute here, Poker Pigeon, you're contradicting yourself. Before, you've said that we should play KQ on the button, and that you should even raise with the hand if no one's raised before you."

I've never said any such thing, though I'm not surprised that you don't remember my exact words, what with everything else I'm throwing at you. One of the most common mistakes that otherwise-competent players make in limit Hold 'Em is to over-value their pocket cards simply because they're sitting on the button or in late position. What I actually said in chapter 4 is that KQ is one of the hands that you *never* play in early position, but that merits a raise where you're sitting in *late* position, if no one's raised before you. But here, one player you've identified as a shark has raised with first action after the big blind, and another Great White has called the raise from the sixth chair. Since you've identified both of these guys as textbook position players, it's safe to assume that the initial raiser has AQ at the minimum and is probably even stronger than that, and that the man in the sixth chair has either a medium pair, medium-size suited connectors, or a couple of fair-size cards, one of which will be an ace or king with the other being a ten or higher. So your KQ is practically drawing dead against the initial raiser, and is very likely behind the player in the sixth chair as well.

Throw this hand away.

So what hands *should* you play in this situation? AA, KK, or AK, of course—that goes without saying no matter what position you're in—but even on the button, when there is a raise and a call before you, you should fold with any of the *terrible* hands listed in chapter 4 (KQ, KJ, K10, or ace-anything other than AK). With your late-position advantage here, it's okay to come in with any *other* two cards, like, say, 78 or 9-10—or even 52, for Christ's sake—as long as you don't keep anything large enough so that if one of your pocket cards happens to match the biggest card shown on the flop, you'll be up against an equal top pair with a bigger kicker than yours. In fact, when you come up with mid-size suited connectors on the button in a situation such as this, you might even *double*-raise. Then if the shark beside the big blind should happen to *triple*-raise, and the guy in the sixth seat calls those two bets, then you'll know you're up against a couple of big-assed pairs. Then you should call the final ten bucks (everything we're talking about in this book assumes a ten-and-twenty game), but if the flop doesn't hit you in two places or give you a straight or flush draw, then you should get away from the hand. And when you've *double*-raised before the flop and neither of your opponents comes back at you, they're probably going to check to you after the flop, and at that point you can get a free card if you need one.

Are you beginning to see the difference between playing position at all times, and *knowing* position play even though you don't always practice it? Where you've identified the self-imagined "real" players in the game, watching their actions before the flop will give you an excellent read on their pocket cards, and if you stray occasionally from accepted position play before the flop, these same sharks will take detailed notes on the hands you show down at the end and think you're a pigeon, and never suspect that you're otherwise.

In connection with the above, lemme throw another postulate atcha, as follows: **If you have a good read on your opponents' hands, you have a monstrous advantage, no matter what position you're sitting in, and getting a good read on someone's pocket cards comes from knowing that person's playing habits, not from observing the way your opponents blink, hold their mouths, scratch their asses, or reach for their chips left-handed or right-handed, or any other bullshit that you might've heard on ESPN.** In a later chapter we'll delve pretty deeply into what fallacies you may have heard about tells, but for now let's just leave it that players who squint at their opponents searching for facial ticks are wasting their time; they'd be much better off evaluating their opponents' overall play than trying to read the stars' alignment or trotting out voodoo dolls and sticking pins in them. *Medium* is a popular television show, but that's all it is, and sudden vision interpretation has no place at the poker table.

So much for play before the flop and how to identify the strength of your opponents' pocket cards by knowing how they play position for now. We'll go on to *after*-the-flop strategy with regard to position, and here you're going to see why I insist that 95 percent of the skill in limit Hold 'Em comes to light only after the first three cards have hit the board.

9

After the Flop

When the Pigeon Spreads Its Wings

Catty-corner across from Columbus Circle sit a row of benches along the sidewalk, in full view of the hicks-from-the-sticks and honest-to-goodness lovers climbing into horse-drawn carriages for tours of Central Park. Or if you're part of the Great Unwashed who've never made it to Central Park, or you wouldn't pay the exorbitant costs and battle the airport security forces in order to get there, I'll lay you odds that there is a similar row of benches in some park or on some square in your hometown. On spring and summer afternoons, park benches across the country support the fannies of people with little paper bags who are feeding popcorn to the pigeons. The pigeons don't seem to have much to do other than peck around, and neither, I might add, do the people.

Anyway, pigeons waddling around pecking for morsels have become such a common sight that the casual stroller will barely notice them, not even looking in their direction unless a bird should take flight with a sudden rush of wings. When that happens the passerby will stop in his tracks to stare, a look on his face that clearly says, *"Jesus Christ, where did all those fuckin' birds come from?"* even though his feathered friends have been right there in plain view all along.

Your own actions when you're playing poker should mirror the park pigeons'. Before the flop you're just waddling and pecking, and while the hustlers might *think* that you don't know what you're doing, after the flop hits the board, you can flap your wings a bit and *convince* them that you're a moron.

For example, Desperate Man and his cohorts know that in early position you should never see the flop without pristine starting cards, yet here the flop comes and you're in the big blind position, and have stood a raise from the on-the-button man with 10-4, both spades, in your hand. All well and good, but if the flop doesn't hit you in at least two places (or unless you can accidentally-on-purpose flash your cards as you toss them in), then you're going to fold, and your stupidity's going to be lost on all of the hustlers. But then all of a sudden, *boom*, the flop comes down something like K♠,6♠,2♠. Such a flop is rare, but it happens.

Now you've got 'em. The real pigeon would figure that the pot is as good as his at this point (even though in fact he's a long way from home free), so here's your chance to try and win a big 'un while playing like a dyed-in-the-wool pigeon just as Analytical Man has you pegged and Desperate Man hopes you are. Your most convincing inept move on the way to raking in this pot will be to employ the worst strategy in Hold 'Em, known for now and evermore as the Weak Player's Fourth Street Check-Raise, but even before that you should make everyone at the table think that they've picked up a tell by staring bug-eyed at the three cards in the center of the table before making any move at all.

Well, okay, that's a bit much. You don't want to sit there bug-eyed with your mouth agape because that posture looks phony as hell, but you do want to exhibit little abnormal twitches of some kind whenever you've stood a raise before the flop in early position with a godawful hand, then have gotten a miracle flop to outstrip the field. I'll suggest one good ploy, though you should really develop your own moves. When I want to exhibit a tell, as soon as the flop hits I'll look at the three faceup cards and murmur, almost under my breath, "King, six, deuce, huh? King, six, deuce," repeating the values of the flop cards a couple of times. Then I'll check. The robotic naming of the flop cards isn't the issue, it's being certain that you repeat this act only when you've flopped a monster, because then and only then will the hustlers be certain that they've picked up a tell. And in fact it *is* a tell, since you'll only be doing it when you're holding the nuts or near-nuts, even though you're really just baiting the hook. You should never put forth your tell and then, a few hands later, show the same tell when you don't have a damned thing. Pigeons exhibit tells and then check *only* when they have a monster hand. Remember that. And with the foregoing in mind, it's now time for a full discussion of **The Weak Player's Fourth-Street Check-Raise,** and why, even though it's among the worst Hold 'Em strategies known to man, it's the best way to look like a pigeon to the experts and still take the money home.

You've flopped a big hand to go with your 10-4, you've put your tell on display, and now you check. Checking in early position after the flop, especially when you've got a big hand and are trotting out the old Weak Player's Fourth-Street Check-Raise trick, requires a little showmanship. Your tone of voice should be, for want of a better term, sort of fakey-hesitant, though the certified pigeonish manner of saying "I check" is really hard to describe. For the best example you can get, try sitting in a casino card room game watching the people who really *are* pigeons. (They're pretty easy to spot; the pigeon is the guy taking a tongue-lashing from Desperate Man after the pigeon has won a pot with some stupid play and Desperate Man has come unglued.) Almost

without exception, whenever the bona fide pigeon flops a monster hand in early position, he's going to check in a quavering
voice, with an expression of despair on his face as if he's leaving
the Bastille on his way to the guillotine. Then, when someone
bets behind him, the pigeon will pretend to think a while before
calling. He might even give his chips a good-bye kiss as he tosses
them into the pot, though he's wasting his time trying to sell
anything other than the fact that he's a really crappy player. The
real players in the game have already put the pigeon on a big
hand the moment he checked, and the fact that he calls after
someone else bets just confirms their suspicions. If the pigeon
were on a draw, he wouldn't have made such a big to-do out of
calling, and if he really has nothing as he's trying to pretend,
then what the fuck is he calling for?

The pigeon's pigeon-like strategy, of course, is to wait until
Fourth Street when the limit doubles, then check-raise and pop
'em for forty bucks (assuming this is a ten-and-twenty game) instead of the ten-per-player he'd have gotten if he'd bet after the
flop. And occasionally, he will score a big pot with this trick—
this generally happens when the game is populated with suckers
whose play is every bit as poor as the pigeon's, if not more so—
just as the guy fishing with a bent pin and an earthworm will
catch a crappie or two but, in the long run, a man with a sophisticated lure will land the biggest bass and take home the prize.

I can't emphasize enough that **There is no worse play in
Hold 'Em than the Weak Player's Fourth-Street Check-Raise.
In my book, the Fourth-Street Check-Raise surpasses even
the no-draw draw (where two cards are needed to make the
hand) or any other lamebrained maneuver you can think of.
But it's also the best weakness that you can exhibit in line
with what we're trying to accomplish, holding you out as a
pigeon when really you're not, because, at least with the Weak
Player's Fourth-Street Check-Raise, you will always get to**

show down your piss-poor pocket cards at the end and you're not going to lose any money overall with these hands. You will lose the occasional pot with this ploy, due to your own poor play, but in the long run you'll actually win a little. It's just that you'll never win half as much as you should with your strong hands, and that's a more serious fault in the pigeon's play than losing more than you ought to with your second-rate holdings.

And if you're sitting there thinking, *Hey, wait a minute; checking a flush after the flop and then popping their asses on Fourth Street sounds like one helluva play,* then you should either go back to the front of this book and start over, or give up Hold 'Em altogether. Limit poker isn't a game of winning big pots. Limit poker is a game of reducing losses in the hands you don't win and maximizing profits in the hands you do. And in case you haven't yet figured it out, besides keeping your opponents off balance with your pigeon moves, it's also a big advantage that while you'll be able to figure out the experts' hands by the plays that they make—since you're also studying what a good player would do in your same situation—the experts will be completely in the dark as to what the fuck you're up to. The so-called Real Player, when flopping a flush, will usually come out betting after the flop and raising the maximum at every opportunity, playing his monster flops *exactly* the same as when he merely flops top pair and is trying to drive players out of the pot before they draw out on him. The expert knows that if he comes out firing in this situation, the weak players won't put him on a monster hand because they'll expect him to slow-play the nuts just as they do. The good players will also have a tough time reading him because he plays every type of hand the same. It will take several years in the trenches before you realize just how bad a play the Weak Player's Fourth-Street Check-Raise happens to be, but let's look at just a few of the pitfalls.

First of all, in the scenario we've just described (the 10-4 of spades in your hand with three spades on the flop), there is a 16 in 47 chance of a *fourth* spade hitting the board either on the turn or the river (go back to "The Oddball Odds of Texas Hold 'Em" if you want to figure this out for yourself), and with your biggest pocket spade being a 10, it's almost a dead certainty that with a four-flush on the board you're going to lose. So if you check this hand after the flop you're giving the other players the chance to check behind you and try drawing out on you for free. And even worse, you're in danger of having this hand drawn out on even if you flop something bigger than a flush, say, a 10,10,4, giving you an instant full house. In that event, any running pair bigger than your 10s will almost certainly cause you to lose to a bigger full house (two running jacks, for example, will give any player with a jack in his hand a bigger full house than yours), and a running pair *in between* 10s and 4s, say, 6s, will give anyone holding the case 10 a split with you. It's true that when you flop a flush or full house you become a major favorite to win, but these hands get drawn out on all the time.

Not only does the Weak Player's Fourth-Street Check-Raise put you in danger of losing the pot altogether through giving free draws, but even when your hand stands up and you win the pot, you're going to give away a lot of profit in the long run. To paraphrase one of the earliest postulates in this book, the good player's strategy is **Never to give anyone a free card when he knows that he has the best hand. If you're first in line, bet. With second or last action, raise. Always.**

And in case you're still in doubt about the Weak Player's Fourth-Street Check-Raise and its position on the Stupid Pet Tricks chart, let's walk through three imaginary hands. In the first example, your Weak Player's Fourth-Street Check-Raise works as well as it possibly can, while in the second you get just the result that you deserve. In the final example, someone will draw out and you'll manage to lose the pot. Let's keep your situation constant in that your pocket cards are 10♠4♠ in each example, you have the big blind seat, the button man has raised before the flop, and you've called along with three Sklansky-disciple, down-the-line position players behind you. And out rolls the same flop that we discussed before, K♠,6♠,2♠. You widen your eyes for an instant (or clear your throat, or swallow hard, or pick your nose, or grab your crotch, or whatever tell you've decided to exhibit), and then you check.

Best-case scenario: One of the position players has a king with a moderate kicker, a jack or ten, and this player, having made top pair, bets. The other two pre-flop callers fold. The guy on the button, who raised before the flop with pocket nines, calls—actually, he calls *only* if he's a really poor player: a fair player would toss his hand in right there, while a good player might raise to test out the bettor's hand, then fold if the bettor comes back over the top with yet another raise—and you, after squinting and scratching your head, call as well. Fourth Street produces the eight of hearts, a total blank for all concerned. You check again. The initial bettor bets again and the button man calls. Now your eyes narrow and you show your teeth in a grin of triumph, pull forty bucks in chips from your stack, and pop their asses. Position-Playing Man, still holding top pair, calls your raise, figuring that he's beat but also thinking that he's gone too far to quit and might even draw out on the end. The button man realizes that he's just seen the old Weak Player's Fourth-Street Check-Raise trick, and tosses his cards away. Fifth Street brings another no-help card. Now you bet. Position Man calls, and you show your flush with pride. Here's what you've won in addition to the pre-flop money: Twenty bucks after the flop, forty bucks on Fourth Street, and twenty bucks on the end, a total of eighty dollars. As you drag the pot, the other players exchange knowing glances. They have a pigeon in their midst.

If they could tie you to your chair to prevent you from escaping at that point, they probably would.

And the above example is the *best*-case scenario. The *usual* case scenario would unfold thusly: While the pre- and post-flop action would be the same as above, when you trot out your heavy artillery on Fourth Street after Position Man bets and the button man calls, *both* of your opponents recognize the Weak Player's Fourth-Street Check-Raise and toss in their hands, leaving you to rake in a forty-dollar profit. This result would be the Just Reward for your amateurish ploy. In either case, you'd get to show your flush (flashing your cards in the second case before you toss them in and saying something like, "I wish you guys had called"), the other players would recognize you as a pigeon, and you'd thus be accomplishing your goal without losing any money.

Now let's talk about the imaginary hand that you lose. In this case, instead of having top pair after the flop, Position Man has the ace of spades with a medium-to-weak kicker, and the flop of K♠,6♠,2♠ leaves him with a draw to the best flush possible. After you tug on your ear—or grab your crotch or, once again, whatever tell you're showing—then check, this man will bet in hopes that he can take the pot then and there should you and the button man fold—and also increase his potential winnings in case another spade should fall. In this imaginary hand, the guy on the button is a much stronger player than in our first two examples and *raises* with his two nines, hoping to find out if he has the best hand. You call, of course, only now you've cold-called not only a bet but a bet *and* a raise, which is such a dead giveaway that you've flopped a monster that you may as well have leaped out of your chair, stripped naked, and tossed your clothing into the pot. Position Man will also call the raise, but now he's seen your action and knows that he must make a flush in order to win. When a blank comes on Fourth Street, you'll check once more, your fingers itching to get in your stack and raise when one of the others bets—but guess what. Both of your opponents know that you're on a monster hand because you called the bet *and* raised after the flop. Both men check behind you, so not only have you gotten your last nickel from your opponents if your hand stands up but you've also given Position Man the opportunity to draw out on you for free. And if a spade hits the board on the end you'll be forced to check, Position Man will bet, the button man will fold, and you'll have to piss off twenty more dollars to "keep Position Man honest" and see his ace of spades. You've played the hand as badly as it could possibly be played, and when you show your 10,4 of spades on the end while cussing your rotten luck at being drawn out on, your opponents will be ready to vote you into the Pigeon's Hall of Fame.

To drive into your head, once and for all, that the Weak Player's Fourth-Street Check-Raise is among the worst Hold 'Em strategies possible, we're going to play one more imaginary hand, only this time we'll play the hand the way it *should* be played. As before, you have 10♠ 4♠ in the pocket in the big blind position, call the button man's pre-flop raise along with three dyed-in-the-wool position players, and then watch the miracle flop of K♠,6♠,2♠ appear. You have first action, and this time you don't gasp, widen your eyes, or adjust your underwear. You reach into your stack with no hesitation whatsoever, and fog ten dollars into the pot.

Now you've created a dilemma for the other players that didn't exist when you tried checking your way onto Fourth Street. If Position Man has a king and medium kicker in the pocket (as was the case in the first and second examples above), he'll raise, and everyone else (including the button man, whose pocket nines are obviously worthless when he's facing a bet *and* a raise) will toss in their hands and leave you head up with Position Man. And you're not through. When it's your turn again you *re*-raise. Five'll get you ten that Position Man will call, or possibly even raise a second time (mainly to test the strength of your hand, in which case you'll cap the betting by exhausting the final raise), but five'll get you *twenty* that he'll pause a long time before he acts at all.

Why? Simple. Where in the previous examples your opponents figured out quickly that you were employing the Weak Player's Fourth-Street Check-Raise, in this instance Mr. Position Man has no idea what you're up to. He thinks that you likely have top pair, just as he does, but he's unsure whether or not you have a better kicker. Under no circumstances does he believe that you're stronger than top pair with a fair kicker, because to have *two* pair you would have called a pre-flop raise with K6, K2, or 62, which no player in their right mind would have done. And you don't have a set (he'll eliminate KK as your pocket cards because you would have re-raised before the flop, but might consider 66 or 22 as possibilities) or a flush (the hand you actually have) because then you wouldn't be playing the hand this strongly out of the chute and would be waiting until Fourth Street before really letting the hammer down. In any event, Position Man is now committed to seeing this hand through 'til the bitter end, even though he's practically drawing dead.

In the same circumstance as in the *third* example above (where you lost the pot), Position Man, holding the ace of spades and drawing to the nuts, will merely call your after-the-flop bet, in which case you'll have the button man (and possibly even one or two more of the position players who've looked at the flop) along for the ride as well. If the button man should test your strength with a raise, you'll immediately re-raise just as you would have if Position Man had raised, but now Position Man, having a draw to the nut flush, will have to call all bets, and the button man will slide a final ten bucks into the pot—even though he now knows for sure that he's beaten—in the faint hope that he can wish a third nine out of the deck on Fourth Street. Since you can also beat three nines, you hope that Button Man hits that third nine and sticks around. Position Man remains your primary threat because he's drawing to beat you if a fourth spade should appear, but you're now getting two-to-one for your money in a hand where you're a prohibitive favorite to win.

So with the preceding paragraph in mind, mark the following down and add it to your notes, and assume that this question will appear on the Final Exam: **Really good players bet their monster hands strongly after the flop just as they would a marginal hand (such as top pair with a pretty good kicker) because the other players will expect them to slow-play the nuts or near-nuts, and will never put the good player on a big hand where, after the flop, the good player immediately takes the lead. You'll get more action by playing your big hands strongly out of the chute than you'll ever realize with the Weak Player's Fourth-Street Check-Raise, and that's why occasional use of the Weak Player's Fourth-Street Check-Raise will do more to convince your opponents that you're a pigeon than any other lame-brained strategy that you can use. Even though you'll give up a lot of profit by slow-playing a few monsters, you'll more than make up for the deficit with the future payoff you'll receive because the other players have no respect for you, and in turn don't respect your hands.**

So much for the Weak Player's Fourth-Street Check-Raise. Before we move on to other amateurish ploys you can use to establish yourself as a pigeon, however, I think it's time to discuss check-raises in general. From the tone of this chapter up to now, you might think that I'm dissing *all* check-raises as poor plays, but really I'm not. Check-raises in general are excellent arsenal components for the player who knows how to use them. It's just that checking and raising at the proper time requires a great deal of thought and a whole lot more skill than a pigeon should have, so rather than using check-raises yourself, you should know when and where a good player might check and raise, and use that knowledge as an additional tool in putting your opponents on hands.

So with the foregoing in mind here's another Pigeon's Postulate, a general, overall statement about checking and raising: **Good players never check and then raise merely in an attempt to increase the size of the pot because there's no guarantee that when they check, someone else is going to bet and give them the opportunity to raise. Also, the most effective check-raise comes** *after the flop,* **not on Fourth or Fifth Street, where the betting limit doubles. Lying in wait until Fourth Street lets all the other players know that the check-raiser has the nuts or near-nuts, and if they're not at least** *drawing* **to the best possible hand, the other guys will toss their cards away. Check-raising after the flop keeps the good player's opponents off balance. If the good player check-raises after the flop, then checks once more on Fourth Street, the other players will worry that if they bet, he's going to raise again. When he check-raises after the flop, he might have a draw, a big kicker to go with top pair, or he could be stone-cold bluffing. Check-raising, like every other play in Hold 'Em, is most effective when the use of it doesn't telegraph the check-raiser's hand to the other players.**

"Wait a minute," you say. "If a good player might check-raise after the flop with just about any kind of a hand, then how can you use his check-raising to figure out what he's got?"

Excellent question—but you didn't let me finish. . . . Here's how.

No matter how many good to championship-quality poker players you might run across in your travels, 999 out of 1000 of them will have one thing in common. There is no sport or game in existence where the Mine's-Bigger'n-Yours mentality exists in stronger form than in Texas Hold 'Em poker, and this is true with the so-called pros as much as it is true with the bona fide pigeons. I can name exactly three players I've met who have the mental toughness to keep ego completely out of their decision-making process. All three of these guys are longtime consistent game dominators, and their lack of ego keeps them off of television, out of the public eye, and heavily in the black where their poker results are concerned. For all the rest of the self-imagined poker wizards that I know there is one ultimate goal, to take what they believe to be their well-deserved positions alongside the Brunsons and Hellmuths and Whatnots of the world, and the best way to put some poker hustler's game on tilt is to beat him a hand or two where you employ easily recognized moronic strategies such as the Weak Player's Fourth-Street Check-Raise. Since it's clear from your play that you're the pigeon, the pro won't be able to resist showing you his thereafter (since you've already shown him yours) so as to prove his superhumanity to the world, and the next time you're in a pot with the guy, if his position in the hand is earlier than yours you can count on seeing him checking, then raising after the flop. He's going to think you're too dumb to figure out what he's doing (and, as always, you should never do anything to change his mind in that regard), and when he's on tilt, he's nearly always going to be stone-cold bluffing—and I would have said "always" instead of "nearly always" if it wasn't for the luck factor; occasionally, under the blind-hog-and-acorn theory, he'll have a really big hand when he takes dead aim in his quest to dominate you, but the times when he isn't bluffing will be few and far between.

And your own counteracting maneuvers? Even simpler. When the poker hustler's on tilt and you're sure he's running bluffs, you maintain your dumb expression while calling him down with just about anything that beats the board. And if you win another pot or two with second or third pair (or even *high card*, for Christ's sake), then he's going to be all the more on tilt—and these are the times when you can really make hay in limit poker games. There is no bigger sucker in poker than the so-called pro who's suddenly on tilt, and you should keep this fact firmly in mind and take full advantage of these opportunities. You may rest assured that if the situation were reversed, the poker hustler would show you no mercy, so there's no reason for you not to return the favor.

A strong word of caution, however: While you should always keep an eye out for the hustlers who've gone over the edge a bit, don't get gapped open (out of control) yourself, because for the most part the hustlers will be better players than you. Keep close track of the hustlers who've recently been the victim of some pigeon maneuvers—those are the guys who will be bluffing when they check-raise. When he's not on tilt, the hustler who check-raises after the flop might have anything from nothing to the nuts, and the best thing for you to do under normal circumstances (unless *you've* got the nuts, of course) is to toss your hand in and not fool around with those guys. Calling down on-tilt hustlers when you've got a weak-to-mediocre hand is the fastest way to make money there is in Hold 'Em, but it's also the fastest way to *lose* money if you're wrong about the hustler's mental condition. As always, the secret to success in disguising your game is to make dumb-looking plays that don't cost you very much money when you lose and really pump up profits when you win.

And with all that said, it's now time to move on to another pigeon's maneuver that you can use to make your niche, a maneuver that's only slightly less effective than the Weak Player's Fourth-Street Check-Raise. This one's a nifty little stunt that I like to call the old "Black Widow Throws Up Her Dress" trick, or simply the "Black Widow ploy" for short, so-called after the treacherous widow's assuming of the standard position for getting screwed when really she's about to put some guy's nuts in a vise.

Every good Hold 'Em player will tell you that strong hands should be played aggressively, and that goes for really good *draws* as well when the draws are played in late position. The word among the pros is that checking in early position, and then calling someone else's bet, is the sap's way of telling the rest of the players that he has no confidence in his hand and that he doesn't know c'm'ere from sic 'em about what in hell he's doing. Aggressive play overall is excellent strategy; not only does aggressive play eliminate the ridiculous draw-out possibilities by narrowing down the field but, if your betting pattern puts enough heat on the players behind you, you'll win some pots by default that you'd otherwise lose.

So what do we Pigeons Who Would Be Winners do to solidify our growing reputations as morons?

Why, we play a few strong hands weakly from early position, of course. We throw up our dresses and spread our legs, and when our opponents take the bait we strangle them with our thighs.

We use the old Black Widow trick sparingly, and we never put this maneuver in play when we've just employed the Weak Player's Fourth-Street Check-Raise, or when we've recently sent Desperate Man stomping away from the table and into the john by winning a pot with ridiculous pocket cards. None of our pigeon maneuvers should come in close proximity so that we won't overdo our perceived penchant for pathetic play. The old Black Widow ploy must stand on its own, set apart in time from our other idiotic plays, and must employ only the most pristine of starting hands.

Such as AK. Or AQ, or AJ—or even A10, or something similar. AA, KK, or QQ won't work in this situation, because anyone who's played Hold 'Em for more than ten minutes—and that includes even the pigeons—knows that you're supposed to raise with big pairs, and the fact that you don't raise would red-flag your outwardly sloppy play as being the hoax that it is. The worst thing you can do in trying to put across an intentionally bad play is to make the whole thing look like a fake. What we want to do is take starting cards that would merit a raise from most of the other players at the table, and merely limp into the pot in early position by calling the big blind plus whatever raises occur along the way. You're going to remember (and would probably point out in a loud voice, if I wasn't bringing the subject up myself) that in an earlier chapter I said you should never play in a raised pot from early position with AJ or A10, and that advice is still right on. But really weak players come in pots with AJ or A10 in early position, and being Willy Weakguy is the act you're trying to sell, so when using the old Black Widow ploy, you should make an exception and come in with some really crappy hands that contain aces. You're looking for a flop that produces an ace or, even better, produces as its highest card something that pairs whatever you're holding to go with your ace. In other words, when you have AJ you want a jack, when your pocket cards are A10 you want a 10 on the flop, and so on and so forth. When you get your desired flop, you check, just as you did when you were using the Weak Player's Fourth-Street Check-Raise, only this particular manner of checking looks quite a bit different.

Laugh if you want to, but the facial expressions that you use in putting these pigeon's ploys across are the most important tools you have for selling your incompetence. In the Weak Player's Fourth-Street Check-Raise, we described your tone of voice when you check as sort of "fakey-hesitant," accompanied by a slight widening of the eyes to telegraph the fact that you've flopped a monster and are trying to be cool about it. But now you haven't flopped a monster; you've flopped what a pigeon would consider a so-so hand, and the mask that you wear this time in checking is entirely different. In using the old Black Widow trick, you want the other players to know that you've flopped a marginal hand and are honestly hesitant about playing with any aggression. So you don't stare bug-eyed at the flop cards, or pick your nose, or grab at your crotch, or any of that crap. You say, "I check," or, better yet, you just say, "check," quickly and in a soft tone, with no hesitation, an inflection in your voice that clearly says to the other players, "I've flopped a really shitty hand, guys, but it might just be strong enough to keep me in the pot." Just as with the Weak Player's Fourth-Street Check-Raise, you need to visit a number of casino card rooms and watch the real pigeons check with their marginal hands so that you can picture the image you want to project, but the method of checking when you're using the old Black Widow trick is much easier to master. In fact, checking when you're in the midst of the Black Widow ploy isn't really playacting, it's an honest and forthright probe to see what the other players might be holding, and says clearly that your hand is so fair-to-marginal that the other players might even drool.

And here you don't have to worry about whether someone bets behind you. With the highest pair on the board, you've probably got the best hand at the moment (in fact that's the whole idea behind the Black Widow maneuver, slow-playing a hand that anyone else at the table would have played aggressively)—so you do want action, but if all the players check behind you, that's okay as well. If you win this pot it's a bonus; what you really want is to show your hand at the end so that everyone will know that you've tried to check yourself into a loser when you should have tried knocking everyone else out of the pot from the get-go. If no one bets, you get to look at a free ticket. If someone bets, you call and proceed to Fourth Street.

In fact, no matter what cards hit the board on Fourth Street or on the end, your action is going to be the same. You're going to check and call all the way through. Just wait until you see the expression of distaste on the other players' faces, especially the man who's been the aggressor all the way through the hand—if there is one—when you show your pocket cards. If you've had the best hand all along and win the pot, all of your opponents are going to think, *Christ, why didn't the dumbass bet his hand? Guy's luckier'n a two-dicked dog that nobody drew out on him.* Your reputation as a fish is going to grow by leaps and bounds whether you win or lose, and if someone drew out on you while you were screwing around checking and calling, that's even better because now the sharps are going to think that you've gotten exactly what you deserve for slow-playing the hand.

The Black Widow ploy is just about as good for building your image as the Weak Player's Fourth-Street Check-Raise, for a couple of reasons. First of all, because you've been checking and calling instead of betting and raising, if someone draws out on you, you're not going to lose very much, and that's the whole idea behind using carefully selected bonehead plays to establish your pigeonship. Once again: the really poor player doesn't lose by starting out weak or employing weak after-the-flop strategy, the really poor player loses his ass by forking over too much money on hands where he has no legitimate chance to win. So our strategy is to exhibit weakness only in pots where we're not going to lose a whole lot of money. Best of all, even if we win the pot and it's smaller than it should be, our pigeon's credentials will continue to shine like a new dime on asphalt paving.

10

Tells Don't Tell—People Do

Picture this: Gary Gamebreaker-Upper, the Northern Ireland Bomb Shelter No-Limit Champ, squares off against Dennis Draw-out, winner of the 1975 Honolulu Deuces Wild Tourney, for all the marbles, the two poker wizards head-up on the Final Table, the last pair standing out of 20,000 entries in the Main Event at the World Series of Poker. Twenty million bucks on the line. The cash in a four-foot pile at one end of the table. The glistening championship bracelet resting atop the pile of money. The dealer ready to roll. You're dying for some chips 'n' dip, but you're frozen in your seat on the sofa. Two pocket cards come facedown to each player. Each rolls his hand up and peeks at his cards, as the table cam looks on.

Gamebreaker-Upper has first action. The Irishman is the current chip leader, though not by much, a hundred thousand or so, peanuts at the final World Series table. He's a rangy drink of water with a full head of curly dark hair, his eyes hidden behind underwater goggles with black lenses. He's sort of the villain in this match, though it isn't quite fair to say so. Gary Gamebreaker-

Upper himself is a pleasant, mild-mannered guy—though he oozes killer instinct at the poker table—and a perfect gentleman. The fans he's brought with him from across the pond are the problem. They're a rowdy bunch, a dozen strong, and they stand up to chant something that sounds like "Ooga, ooga, booga" in unison every time their hero wins a hand. The two women in the group wear inch-thick rouge and lipstick, tight jeans, and low-cut tops. One of the men has a patch over one eye, and another wears a cloth headband and is bare-chested under a sleeveless leather vest. There's a gun show downtown, and the group from Ireland spends their time away from the poker tournament looking longingly at Uzis and AK-47s. As Gary Gamebreaker-Upper peeps at his pocket cards, the camera pans to the Irish folk. The guy in the leather vest sneers. Then it's back to the table-cam view as Gamebreaker-Upper looks over the queen of hearts and the jack of clubs. He calls the big blind with a deft motion, dividing one stack of chips into two equal stacks, and then pushing both stacks to the center of the table.

Now the table-cam switches over to Dennis Drawout's point of view. Drawout's a portly man in his fifties wearing a Golden Nugget cap, dark sunglasses, and a Clinton-for-President T-shirt, a genuine relic from the early nineties. He's the crowd favorite according to the TV announcers, a great player who's never won since his '75 Honolulu victory, even though many of his peers rate him as the best cash game player alive. His entourage includes four loyal women and eight sturdy men, well-mannered poker fans not given to boisterous celebrations, and they're just as responsible for Drawout's popularity as Gamebreaker-Upper's supporters are responsible for their man's lack of it. There's a lot behind the scenes in the Drawout camp that the television audience isn't aware of; the four female Dennis Drawout fans are in reality Drawout's ex-wives, all desperate for their past-due child support, and the eight men seated along with the women are the guys who've put up Drawout's entry fee. These guys' intense interest in the tournament's outcome has nothing to do with their brotherly love for Drawout. They're each in for a cut of the action, and have flown in to Las Vegas for the express purpose of protecting their investment.

And, oh, yes, there's another tidbit of information about Dennis Drawout that neither the TV audience *nor* his entourage is aware of. In raising the cash to enter the tournament, Drawout sort of overextended himself; in dire need of money to live on, he raised *twenty* thousand dollars from his backers instead of the ten thousand needed to buy in, and assumed that he'd never make it past the first day of the championship because in thirty previous World Series he never had. And now, with the bracelet in sight and 200 percent of the buy-in raised, Drawout's on the horns of a dilemma; no matter how much he wins, he's going to owe his backers twice that amount less his own cut, which is 20 percent. All through the final days of the championship, Drawout's looked thoughtfully off into space every time it's been his turn to act on his hand, and the TV announcers have constantly pointed out Drawout's staring into space as an example of his uncanny ability not to exhibit tells. The truth is, however, that Drawout's constantly looking toward the exit onto Fremont Street because he's wondering, if he should win all the marbles, how much of the cash he can grab as he makes a mad dash for it with his backers and ex-wives in hot pursuit. He turns up the corners of his pocket cards and shows the nine and ten of spades to the table-cam.

Drawout reaches for his stack, sets a pile of chips on the table, returns them all to his stack, puts the chips back on the table, then puts them away a couple of times more, and—as Norman Chad points out to the world that Drawout always fools with his chips exactly three times before acting on his hand—finally comes up with a two-hundred-thousand-chip raise. Gamebreaker-Upper calls with no hesitation. The dealer knocks once on the table, burns one, deals three cards facedown, then turns them up side by side. The flop is on the board and the action is underway.

Ace of diamonds, king of clubs, three of clubs. No help to either man.

Gary Gamebreaker-Upper adjusts his swimming goggles, taking his time about it; then, aggressive as always, he makes a bet of four hundred thousand chips. His chip count totals over twelve million, so four hundred thou's not that much, but it is enough to give his opponent pause.

You desperately need to go to the bathroom, but you're not about to move. You grab the remote and adjust the volume.

Dennis Drawout tilts his Golden Nugget cap back on his head and pushes his sunglasses upward until they rest just below the bill of his cap. As Gary Gamebreaker-Upper stares him down, Drawout props one knee against the edge of the table and folds his arms. His pale blue eyes widen slightly as he sets his gaze on something off in the distance, in the general direction of the exit onto Fremont Street.

And Norman Chad says to Lon McEachern, "This is all for show, Lon. No way can Dennis call this bet with ten high and both an ace and a king on the board, but he wants Gary to think he's really got something and is considering a call. Remember, Dennis has stared off into space in the exact same manner since Day One of the tournament. And as for Gary, he thinks he's running a bluff, but he's got the best hand right now, as well as a draw to the nut straight if a ten should hit the board. Dennis can win with a nine and only a nine, and that's if a queen, jack, or ten doesn't fall on the turn or on the river."

No sooner are those words out of Chad's mouth than Dennis Drawout takes his knee off the edge of the table and sets his foot on the floor. Down come the sunglasses to cover his eyes. He adjusts his cap until the bill hovers just over his nose. Drawout puts both hands behind his mountain of chips and makes a forward sweeping motion. "All in," Drawout says.

Your mouth is suddenly dry.

And Norman Chad says, "I can't believe that Dennis is making this play, Lon. There's just not that much in the pot, though he may have picked up a tell on Gary. As you know, players at this level are phenomenal at reads—that's the only reason Dennis could possibly be playing the hand this way. Gary can't possibly call this bet, even though he's got the winning hand right now. Dennis is going to win the pot by default, but it's not going to be enough money to justify the risk. As I said, I just don't understand Dennis's logic here."

You've seen both hands with the benefit of the table-cam, and you can't fault Chad's logic. Gamebreaker-Upper's going to fold and thus give Drawout a tiny chip lead. Both players have risked more than they should've with two pretty lousy hands.

Gary Gamebreaker-Upper stares across the table at Dennis Drawout, who nervously laughs. Gamebreaker-Upper lifts a foot-high stack of chips off of his pile, divides the stack in half and performs a one-handed chip shuffle. Drawout continues to laugh, though it's obvious that he's trying not to. Gamebreaker-Upper finally says, "I call. Okay, I call."

Norman Chad's in shock, and his tone of voice shows it. "Lon, that may be the greatest call in the history of poker. I still can't believe it. Talk about nerve. Gary's just called down Dennis in what's probably going to be the final hand of the Main Event, with only *queen high*. How could he have possibly known that he has the best hand? What a *read*, Lon. And now the only way Dennis can win the pot is with a nine. I'm speechless, Lon."

Onscreen, Gary Gamebreaker-Upper turns his pocket cards faceup, a strange smile of confidence on his face. You're as stunned as Norman Chad. Christ, how did he know? Gary Gamebreaker-Upper has to be the greatest player in the history of the . . .

But wait a minute.

Gamebreaker-Upper's gaze lowers until he's looking at the pocket cards he's just laid out. His confident expression dissolves into a look of pure horror. He slaps his forehead with his palm. "Oh, lord, I've misread my hand. I thought I had a king in the pocket." His voice sounds faint and far away.

Dennis Drawout's chin is now practically touching his chest. "Good call," he says with a brief nod, then exposes his 9-10 for all the world to see.

Gary Gamebreaker-Upper stares at Drawout's pocket cards. He rubs his eyes. Then his confident look returns. "I *knew* I'd picked up a tell. I was pulling your bloody leg, Denny; I never thought I had a king. Bloke's played poker as long as I have, you think he could misread his hand?"

The dealer places both sets of pocket cards on the table above the flop cards. He burns and turns. A three. He burns and turns again. A four. Irish hero Gary Gamebreaker-Upper has conquered the field to win the World Series of Poker. He lifts his arms skyward like an official signaling a touchdown. In the background, his fans stand, shake their fists, and shout in unison, "Ooga, ooga, booga," one final time.

Norman Chad battles his way through the throng of well-wishers, takes Gary Gamebreaker-Upper by the arm, and shoves a microphone in the winner's face. "First of all, Gary," Chad says, "I want to congratulate you on this phenomenal feat. Tell us. What does this victory mean to you?"

Gamebreaker-Upper looks confused. "Beg pardon?"

"All this money," Chad says, "what does it mean to you?"

"Not as much as the bracelet means, Norman. The money's nice, though. Means I can help the cause back home."

"Oh? What cause is that?"

Gamebreaker-Upper doesn't answer. His entourage has formed

a semi-circle behind him. He gives them a wink. They all collapse in laughter.

"I'll tell you, Gary," Chad goes on, unruffled, "That last hand,
that's the greatest read I've ever seen. How did you do that?"

"Bloke has a tell, Norman. A loud bloody tell."

"And what you said about misreading your hand and thinking you had a king. That was just you giving Dennis the needle,
right?"

"Yeah, yeah. Just a little sport I was having with the man. No
one thinks a man with my experience could possibly misread his
hand."

"Of course not," Chad says. "If you can share it with the television audience, exactly what tell did you pick up that caused you
to call that last bet?"

Gamebreaker-Upper's head turns slightly in a cagey look. "I
don't suppose it matters now, Norman, though I wouldn't have
let this out while the tournament was going on. It's the way he
studies. Man's debating his play, he takes off his sunglasses and
stares into space. Anytime a man won't look you in the eye, he's
bloody bluffing."

"Who'd have thought? Those lingering looks toward the exit,
right?"

"Right, Norman. Hey, the game's here on the table, not out
in the street."

"Well, let's get Dennis in here," Chad says, "to see what he
has to say about it. Second place money's not bad, really."

"No, it's not. But the bracelet doesn't come along with it."

"Right." Chad looks off-camera. "Dennis Drawout. Could you
come in here and tell us . . . ?" Now Chad looks confused. "Well,
where did he go?"

"Beats me, Norman," Gamebreaker-Upper says. "As soon as the
hand was over he made for the exit. Ran down Fremont Street with
some women on his trail. Must be quite a lover."

"Must be," Chad says. "Or maybe he just needed some air."

Heard in the background, one of the security guards hovers over the first-prize money as he yells, "Hey, some of this money's gone. What in hell is happening here?"

If the above fictional scenario sounds far-fetched, then you haven't been around many of these big-time poker tournaments. For a dead broke to limp to the final table with bill collectors and loan sharks on his heels is an every-year occurrence, and for a man holding himself out to be a professional poker player to misread his hand is common as well—and the last part isn't a slam against the players for the misread; anyone who plays poker eight to twelve hours a day for weeks on end eventually experiences bouts of double vision, and it's a miracle that misreads don't happen more often than they do. And as for the television stars that go to great lengths to explain how they pick up tells from their opponents' body language, I've got just one word for them.

Baloney.

And here I go again, making enemies right and left among the poker elite. I'm sorry, but I just can't help it. The mystique of tells makes for good showbiz, and the covering up of tells is the reason that players give for all of the State Trooper/Intimidator sunglasses and goofy-looking headwear seen around these tournaments, but the idea of people having the power to read players' minds by the way they sit, move their eyes, reach for their chips, or scratch their asses belongs right alongside Superman's X-ray vision—straight from Krypton, great funnybook material, and perfect let's-pretend fantasy vehicles for retards and five-year-olds.

So if you're one of the poker players who suffers from what I call the I'm-Kreskin-in-Disguise Syndrome, I can only offer apologies if I'm bruising your ego, but I'm still not backing down from my position. Please listen up. If I didn't think I had something important to say, I'd cut this chapter from the book.

So are there really players whose pocket cards are obvious from the way that they're playing these hands?

Of course there are.

Well, if that's true, isn't developing the ability to pick up tells on other players one of the most important steps in moving your game up to the professional level?

Nope. Not by a long shot. Let me explain.

Actually, the good players that you see on television will claim to disagree with what I'm saying here, but really, after they think about it and cuss me for a while, most of them will agree in spades. Their story for public consumption is that, while they can pick up tells on the weaker players, the real pros are nearly impossible to read.

Okay, I'll buy into that theory, at least to a certain extent. You can read the bona fide pigeons with relative ease, but that won't extend to Analytical Man and his crew because they're good players, even if they're not professionals on the Brunson/Hellmuth/Harrington level. Where I differ strongly from what you hear on TV is in the *method* of reading players, not in the result. The players that you can read easily are so inept that you don't really need to pick up any tells on them: they're going to waste so much money playing poker that reading them isn't a necessary part of moving their money from their pockets into yours.

And as for the so-called professionals, it's true that it's difficult if not impossible to pick up tells on them, but their inscrutability has nothing to do with all of these staring contests that you see on television. I'm talking about the times when two guys lock gazes through their sunglasses and sit motionless until one of them starts giggling, which is the same game you used to play with your friends in *grammar school*, for Christ's sake! The television producers strain a gut in trying to put the idea across that he who giggles first is the one tipping his hand. The fact that a large number of laymen swallow all that crap just proves the old adage that we're a nation of sheep, and also provides backup for H.L. Mencken's idea that no one ever went broke underestimating the intelligence of the American people.

Try this experiment. The next time you're in extended poker-watching mode, get a pad and pen, and keep track of the various staring contests. You should have columns giving the names of the players involved, the exact length of the contest (have a stopwatch along when you do this), the name of the player who giggles first, and finally, the name of the player who either folds his hand or loses the pot after a show of pocket cards. I'll bet you a dollar to a doughnut that over a period of time and over a number of sessions, Mr. Giggle-First has the same number of checks in the win column as Mr. Stoneface.

And here's another little exercise for you. During each telecast, the announcers are going to tell you which players are the pros and which players are the pigeons (although they'll use terminology for the pigeon that's more politically correct, such as "top-flight amateur," or "first-time tournament participant"), so you won't have any trouble identifying these parties. Make a pigeons-only list and, while the telecast is going on, watch these people and these people only, and every time they place a bet watch their actions. Some will bet with their left hands one time and their right hands the next. Others will play with sunglasses on at times and sunglasses off at others. Hats will be tilted back or pulled down low over their eyes, depending on their mood. They'll fiddle with their noses or rest their chins on lightly clenched fists, or tug on their ears Carol Burnett style. In this exercise you should make careful note of these little mannerisms, and also note whether, when the mannerism appeared, the player was bluffing, not bluffing, or preparing to fold or call or raise or whatever, then see if you can predict what that player is going to do in the future based on the mannerism repeating itself.

Guess what. You won't have a clue what the guy's up to ninety-nine times out of a hundred. Bet you your next championship bracelet against my last one that you won't.

And guess what else. In the rare cases where you will be able to predict a player's actions based on some mannerism's repeating itself, when the mannerism next appears, your prediction of the player's next move will be wrong. Therefore, the tell that you thought you'd picked up isn't a tell at all, and the fact that the player was bluffing the first and second times that the so-called tell appeared is merely a coincidence.

And finally: Even where you find a player whose mannerisms are such good predictors that you know in advance what he's going to do every single time, these tells will be of zero assistance to someone trying to win the World Series of Poker. There are five thousand participants in the World Series and, as the field shrinks by elimination, players rotate regularly from table to table. Say you were a player, and say you'd picked up a tell on around five tourney participants (and that number would be just about all that even the big-time pro could keep up with), the odds against you ever facing one of these players in a showdown hand would be astronomical. And even if you should face one of these guys head-up on the final table with twenty million bucks on the line, the chances would be slim that the outcome would hinge on the particular tell that you've spotted. The final hand in virtually every championship involves two players with big hands shoving it all in the center, with the winner being the guy who's lucky enough to have the stronger of the two primo hands. Tells don't matter a whit in these instances, since any poker player in the world would risk it all if he or she had either player's hand at that particular time.

What follows is my favorite lesson on picking up tells on players, and yes, I know that this example is drawn from a World Series no-limit event and I've told you that you should stick to the limit cash games. But effective analysis of other players' pocket cards is exactly the same whether you're playing two-bit limit or as high as gasoline, so I've picked an example from a hand that you may have seen on television.

Once or twice a week, ESPN Classics shows poker championships of old, and if you've never seen it, be sure to tune in to the 2003 World Series Final between Sam Farha and Chris Moneymaker the next time that it's on. Norman Chad and Lon McEachern will let you know in a hurry that Moneymaker was the pigeon and Farha was the pro (which was true: Sam Farha's a longtime poker wizard from the Houston area while Moneymaker had never played in a tournament before and had won his seat through an Internet tourney where his original buy-in was forty bucks), and that the only reason Moneymaker'd made it this far was by his dumb-lucky draw-outs as the cards ran over him all week long (true as well; Moneymaker's catching, on the next-to-last tournament day, of one of the remaining three aces in the deck to knock out Phil Ivey was as bad a beat as I've ever seen with that much money on the line).

In the end Moneymaker took home all the marbles in typical pigeon-on-a-roll fashion, by taking a 45 up against Farha's J10 and getting the miracle flop of J,4,5, but the final hand in the tournament was by no means the *pivotal* hand. *That* hand occurred a few deals earlier, when Sam Farha came into a pot with Q9 against Moneymaker's K10. Moneymaker's pocket cards were a slight favorite over Farha's going in, of course, and Moneymaker made a token raise before the flop that Farha called. The flop produced a 9 as its high card, and two small tickets that were of no help to either player.

Farha checked his top pair and Moneymaker checked as well,

and pro that Farha is, I question his after-the-flop strategy to this very day. His pair of nines was clearly the best hand at the time unless Moneymaker held a pocket pair higher than nines. A lone pair of nines is hardly a trap-setting hand, so instead of giving Moneymaker a free look at the turn card, Farha should have made a fairly strong bet from early position, say a hundred and fifty thousand. If he had, Moneymaker likely would have folded. And even if Moneymaker had come over the top bluffing with a raise, Farha could have tossed in his cards and saved himself from the disaster that the hand eventually became.

The turn produced another card that was smaller than a nine, leaving Farha still in the driver's seat with the top pair to go with his queen kicker, though the Fourth Street card was the third spade to hit the board. Since the top card in Moneymaker's hand was the king of spades, Moneymaker now had a big flush draw and could win the pot with a king, a ten, or another spade on the river, though he was still far behind in the hand.

Sam Farha then made the bet that I believe he should've made after the flop, a hundred and fifty thousand. Moneymaker studied for a short while before announcing a raise. He then put his own hundred and fifty thou in the pot to match Farha's bet and added five hundred thousand chips of his own.

Farha called with no hesitation, and here I'm going to question his strategy again— (Look, I know that this chapter is supposed to be about getting tells on players, and by now you're thinking that you could do without my railbird's-eye-view critique of Farha's play, but please bear with me and I'll tie all of this stuff together in just a few more paragraphs.) To my way of thinking, Farha should have either thrown in his hand or gone all-in right then and there, and I think strongly that going all-in would have been the wiser of the two moves. If Farha had gone all-in, Moneymaker likely would have folded, or if he hadn't folded, he would have made the world's loosest call with nothing but a draw. Farha might've thought that Moneymaker had two pocket spades—and if he actually thought that his opponent had a flush, he should've folded, but as we'll see in a moment, Moneymaker's playing of the hand to that point pretty much eliminated that possibility.

The 2003 World Series of Poker was by no means Sam Farha's first rodeo. He's normally a staunch Brunson disciple, adhering to the philosophy that checking and calling in Texas Hold 'Em is akin to coyly waiting for a hot babe to give you a kiss when, truth be told, your best buddy is banging her brains out every night. Farha's normally aggressive style renders his play in this hand even more puzzling. Folding after Moneymaker's Fourth Street raise would have saved him the half-million chips it cost to call, and would've restricted his loss to the hundred and fifty thousand he'd shoveled in from first position when the turn card had hit the board. And moving all of his chips into the center—as I believe he should've done—would have ended all action on the hand since both players would have been out of chips, and, even had Moneymaker called, would've eliminated the dilemma that Farha faced a moment later when the river card turned out to be *(bugles and drumroll)* . . .

The Ace of Hearts.

Now Sam was really in a pickle. There were already three spades on the board and Moneymaker could've made a flush on the turn, though as I said before, if Farha had really analyzed Moneymaker's play in the hand he would've eliminated that possibility. If Moneymaker had only one spade in his hand (which really was the case) and had missed his flush, then, because Moneymaker had raised before the flop, Farha had to figure him for two big cards in the pocket, one of which very well might have been an ace.

Farha once again threw up his dress and checked to the rookie.

Moneymaker declared himself all-in, making a ballsy stone-cold bluff without so much as a pair.

And now we come to the reading-players-by-body-language versus reading-players-by-their-playing-habits part of the chapter. Yep, it may have taken a while, but I'm finally getting around to my original subject matter. Those of you who've been dozing, listen up.

Sam Farha took a near-world-record amount of time before acting on Moneymaker's all-in bet. He played with his chips. He grinned at Moneymaker in an apparent attempt to get the raw tournament rookie to snicker or giggle or something. He asked Moneymaker in a chiding tone if he'd missed his flush, and then watched Moneymaker a full minute for a reaction before asking the question a second time. Through it all, Moneymaker sat there stone-faced, sunglasses snugged up on his nose, hat pulled low to shade his eyes, and never moved a muscle.

(Even though I don't buy into the read-your-opponents-by-the-way-they-scratch-their-asses theory, I do want to comment on Moneymaker's demeanor in as far as it bolsters my own argument that tells don't tell, but people do. Moneymaker exhibited no tell whatsoever in this instance, but *the fact that he showed no tell was a tell in itself.* Since I watched this hand on TV, I've had a chance to see the entire ESPN broadcast of the 2003 World Series Main Event and therefore have the benefit of seeing Moneymaker play hands that Sam Farha didn't observe, because Farha was playing at another table at the time. When playing previous hands, Moneymaker had a relaxed manner about him, and there was even one instance where, when it came Moneymaker's turn to act, he announced sheepishly that he hadn't even realized that he was still in play and had cards in his hand. When he drew out on Phil Ivey on the way to the Final Table, Moneymaker played with a sort of gee-whiz grin on his face and, when his Fifth Street miracle occurred, he went into a loud cheering-and-hugging-his-mom routine and pumped his fist at the crowd. It's common among inexperienced players to have read a lot of books and to have listened to a lot of professionals' bullshit about getting tells on other players, but when they're actually at the table, novices never think about covering any tells until they're about to bluff and are afraid that someone's going to know it.)

Postulate: **Weak or inexperienced poker players almost never assume rigid poker faces unless they are bluffing. It takes a great deal of practice and experience to maintain the same demeanor at all times when playing poker, and the only reason that this particular postulate isn't locked safely into the Pigeon's safe-deposit box along with the other Pigeon's Postulates for Posterity is that this postulate isn't true 100 percent of the time.** The exceptions, however, are few and far between. If Sam Farha had been observing Moneymaker since the tournament's beginning, he probably would have noticed the difference in the rookie's posturing, but until Farha reached the final table I doubt that he'd ever seen or heard of the guy before.

Sam Farha wasn't the only person in the room who was trying to pick up a tell on Moneymaker during the pivotal hand. Chris Moneymaker's parents were present, seated in the gallery, and during Sam Farha's long and tedious study of their son's all-in move, TV cameras and mikes focused on the couple. Dad Moneymaker concentrated on reading Farha while Mom Moneymaker kept tabs on Chris, and their consensus was that (1) Chris Moneymaker wasn't bluffing and (2) since Sam Farha was fooling with his chips with his left hand instead of his right, he was going to fold. The Moneymakers batted .500. Farha did eventually toss his cards in, but Chris Moneymaker didn't even have a pair and could've won only if his bluff worked and Farha gave up the pot.

My point? Well, as usual, there are a couple of points; they are: (1) I haven't the slightest idea whether or not Sam Farha folds whenever he fiddles with his chips left-handed, and I'd have to watch him for weeks on end to make up my mind about that, but even if he does exhibit a tell *after* the cards are all dealt and it's his turn to call, that knowledge would be totally useless in figuring out how to play the guy *during* the hand. (2) If Chris Moneymaker's *own mother* couldn't figure out whether or not her son was bluffing, how in hell was *Sam Farha* supposed to?

As I said previously, based on his failure to pick up any sort of physical tell after Moneymaker went all-in, Farha threw in his cards. There was over a million in chips in the pot because of the heavy Fourth Street action, and winning that hand gave Moneymaker such a substantial chip lead that a few hands later, he had the luxury of being able to come into a pot with 45 as his pocket cards, made two pair on the flop up against Farha's top pair, and walked away with the bracelet along with two and a half million in prize money. And as for Farha, had he won the pivotal hand either by going all-in on the turn or calling Moneymaker's bet on the end, the championship would have been pretty much over and Farha would have won.

Spilt milk, right? No use to cry over it.

Well, maybe, but in case you're not already sick enough of my talking about this hand, we're going to go over it one more time. Only this time we're going to substitute you for Sam Farha, and instead of waiting for Chris Moneymaker to pick his nose or tug on his ear so that we can get a tell, we're going to base our assessment of Moneymaker's pocket cards on the way he *plays* the hand. Forget Moneymaker's looks or the way he holds his head or peeks at his cards. In fact, in this case, pretend that this is Internet play and you can't even see the guy. You've never met Mr. Faceless across the table, and other than the handle "Moneymaker" printed on his cyberspace chair at this cyberspace poker table, you've never even heard of him, and for all you know he's really a computerized robot.

You are head-up, either with a person named Moneymaker or with this computerized bot, and twenty million buckaroos are on the line. You have Q9 in the pocket. Cyber-space Moneymaker's raised prior to the flop, and you've called. The flop produces 9,4,2, with two spades. You check. (Since you already know that I don't agree with Farha's strategy in playing this hand, I won't stick in my ten-cent critique any farther than I already have— other than to say that since we're trying to read Moneymaker by the way he *plays* his cards, and since we need for Moneymaker to play his hand just as it happened in real life, we're going to duplicate Farha's actions straight down the line. Moneymaker's hand is the king of spades and an off ten, just as before, though in this scenario we're pretending not to know his pocket cards.).

Moneymaker checks after the flop just as you did.

So what have we learned so far?

Well, we're fairly certain that Moneymaker doesn't have an over-pair (10s or higher) because if he did he would have bet the hand. 9,4,2 is a primo flop to 10-10, JJ, QQ, KK or AA, and with any of those pocket holdings Moneymaker would try to put the heat on in an attempt to force you out of the pot and eliminate all draw-out possibilities. He'd also bet with any 9 in his hand, since a 9 would give him top pair just as you have, and in view of the fact that he raised prior to the flop you'd have to put him on a bigger kicker than your queen. And ditto if he had two pocket spades because he might win the pot here and now by betting and wouldn't have to draw for his flush. And even if you called his bet, he's thinking that you'll check to him after Fourth Street arrives, and that he's going to buy himself a free draw in case a spade doesn't come on the turn. So after the flop you already have Moneymaker's pocket cards pretty well isolated; he either has a pair lower than 9s, or he has two unpaired over-cards.

So much for the play after the flop. Are we now ready to look at the turn card?

Nope, because a skillful player will not only try to analyze his opponent's hand, he'll try to get a read on what his opponent thinks that *his own* pocket cards might be. Since you've checked with a 9 as the top card showing on the board, he can't possibly put you on two 9s, the hand that you actually have. So while you played the flop poorly, the hand isn't yet a disaster because you have managed to conceal what pair you do hold.

Now we can look at the turn card. As in real life, it's another card smaller than a 9, and it's a spade.

You're kicking your own ass for not betting after the flop at this point, just as Sam Farha probably was. You fire a hundred and fifty thousand chips into the pot. Moneymaker calls your one-fifty and raises half a mil.

At first you feel a surge of anger directed at yourself, because you fear that your checking after the flop has permitted Money-maker to draw out on you for free. But then you force yourself to cool down and think. Could the small ticket that's just hit the table possibly help your opponent's hand? Well . . .

The answer is found in asking a tough question, one that ninety out of a hundred poker players would answer incorrectly. Here it comes: Has anything happened, including Moneymaker's half-million chip raise on the turn, to change your mind about what his pocket cards might be? Close your eyes, now, and don't cheat. Do you have your answer firmly in mind? Great. Now open your eyes and look at the correct answer below.

Answer: Not one single thing has happened to change your opinion of your opponent's pocket cards; in fact, you now have an *even better* idea of what he's holding. Since he raised a full half-mil, his strategy here can only be a knee-jerk reaction to what he thinks that *you* have. He's certain that you don't have a 9 in the pocket because you didn't bet after the flop (he's wrong, of course). The turn card hasn't helped you unless it's made you a pair smaller than 9s, so either you're betting on a really weak pair or you're out-and-out bluffing. So he raises a sizeable amount to try and knock you out of the pot. He probably wouldn't raise without some draw possibilities, so you have to put him on a big spade. Remember, though, no way does he have a made flush as yet because if he'd had two spades in the pocket he would've bet his flush draw after the flop. The only other possibility is that he's made a set, either on the flop or on the turn, and is slow-playing, but if he had that big a hand he would merely have called on the turn—or possibly would have raised a token amount in order to suck you in. When you call his half-a-million-chip raise you confuse him, since he expected you to either fold or put him all-in. Likely, he thinks, you have a big spade just as he does. No matter what he thinks, you can be 99 percent certain that you have the best hand right now.

And just as you're feeling as if your two 9s might actually win the pot, Fifth Street produces the ace of hearts.

This is where no-limit poker really differs from limit, because you're pot-committed here and Moneymaker wouldn't be able to bet enough on the end in limit poker that you wouldn't risk a call. I can't stress enough how important it is in no-limit poker to get all of the betting done before Fifth Street appears wherever you can. If you'd gone all-in on the turn as you should have, you would have probably already won the pot by default. Even if Moneymaker had called you with his flush draw, you wouldn't have to worry about the ace that has now appeared. Win or lose, all you'd have to do is show your hand.

But now you've got to decide what the chances might be that one of Moneymaker's over-cards is an ace. Since you've been holding your dress up in *fuck-me* posture ever since the hand began, any bet that you make now will be a bluff as obvious as Dolly Parton's knockers, so you check.

Moneymaker declares all-in.

Do you see what I mean about getting all of the action out

of the way in no-limit poker before the river card appears? If you'd gone all-in on the turn, you wouldn't have this godawful decision to make. If you'd stuck to limit poker—as you should have just as you should've gone all-in on the turn, Mr. Pigeon-Out-of-Your-League—then whether you called or not wouldn't be a going-broke decision if you were wrong.

So you sit there staring at that cyber-chair labeled "Money-maker" as goose bumps the size of spider eggs parade up and down your backbone. If you could see your opponent, the way he tilts his head or holds his mouth might give you a clue. Should you call or should you fold?

But wait a minute. In the previous scenario you *could* see Moneymaker, yet you still didn't know what in hell you should do.

So forget the way that Moneymaker might look. Let's consider how he's played the hand. He raised before the flop. After the flop, when you checked to Moneymaker, he checked as well, and right there you put him on two over-cards. The betting on the turn has you convinced that you were right, that Money-maker's pocket cards are unpaired and both are larger than nine. The problem is that an ace fits into that category, and the river card happens to be an ace.

So, does Moneymaker have an ace in the pocket or doesn't he? Sam Farha, facing the same dilemma, decided to toss in his cards.

Your decision here, oddly enough, has nothing to do with Moneymaker's potential hand but everything to do with your reading of *Moneymaker's* reading of *your* pocket cards. Since you checked after the flop, on Fourth Street, and even after the river card hit the table, he can't possibly put you on two 9s, the hand that you have. He thinks you're on a weak pair, or that you have absolutely nothing and were drawing for a flush just as he was. So your decision comes down to two questions that you must

ask yourself: (1) How would Moneymake
in the pocket? and (2) How would he
was bluffing?

The answer is really simple, so in the form of a
to throw you another Postulate from the Poker Pigc
lows:

No novice or even fair-to-middling player goes all-in co
after the river card has appeared unless they are bluffing
("cold" meaning with first action, or with last action when no
one has bet before him). **If they think that they have the best**
hand and are therefore looking for action, they will bet an
amount that won't break their opponent if he calls. If they
have the nuts and think their opponent has a big hand as well,
they still won't go all-in until their opponent commits him-
self. He who shoves his entire stack in the center where his
opponent has showed weakness throughout the hand wants
the opponent to fold. Occasionally the expert will go all-in cold
with a big hand because he knows that if he does, his opponent
will put him on a bluff and likely call, but that situation is so
rare that it shouldn't even be discussed here.

In this regard, I often think of another TV hand I watched
once upon a time, this one between a couple of fair-to-middling
players, T.J. Cloutier and Howard Lederer, both prime-time-type
Hold 'Em guys. The venue was some superstars-only event, one
where the audience wouldn't have to suffer through Uncle Fudd
from Frisco's draw to an inside straight and instead could watch
the heavyweights make a few stupid plays of their own. Cloutier
had first action, and while I clearly recall that Lederer's pocket
cards were KJ, I don't remember Cloutier's exact hand other than
that he had unpaired pocket cards smaller than ten. The flop produced nothing of help to either player, so Lederer continued to
have the best hand. Cloutier checked, and Lederer checked behind him. The turn card was another blank, of aid to no one.

tier shoved all of his chips to the center in an all-out, though advised, bluff, with nothing in the pot other than the pre-flop oney.

Even though Lederer only had king-high, he took a long, long time before folding. Finally he said, "I think that I have the best hand" (which he did) "but I suppose I have to fold." In other words, the second that Cloutier went all-in in first position with only the pre-flop money in the pot, Lederer knew that his opponent was stone-cold bluffing. The problem was that Lederer wasn't sure that his king-jack high could beat even a bluff, and I think to this day that if Lederer had been holding so much as two deuces in the pocket, he would have called and Cloutier would have bluffed his way into an early exit.

As for your decision whether or not to call Computer-Bot Moneymaker's all-in bet, you may rest assured that if Moneymaker held a pocket ace he would be 100 percent sure that he had the best hand, and his mouth would be watering for you to call as much as he could get you to call. He has you on a really weak hand and doesn't think you can possibly call his all-in bet, so he's bluffing his fanny off.

You call. You win. End of example.

I hope that the point of this exercise is getting clearer to you. You couldn't read the human Moneymaker by watching for physical quirks, but you could read the *computerized* Moneymaker by considering the way that he played his hand. In this example, the computerized Moneymaker has played the pot just as a competent Hold 'Em player would, and you've read him successfully because of your knowledge of competent play.

Now, let's take this player reading a step farther. Let's transform the computerized Moneymaker back into a human being, change his name to Mortimer, and assume he's someone that you've played with a hundred times before, not someone you just met while playing in a poker tournament. Also we'll switch the

game to limit poker because that's the game that we're really trying to learn. Mortimer's an average player who goes on tilt fairly
easily, and when on tilt he gives money away by the bushel bas-
ketful. From your experience in playing with the guy, you know
that he always goes over the edge after two or three draw-out beats,
and in this game someone drew out on him just three hands
ago, and a couple of hands before that another player flopped out
on Mortimer's aces in the pocket. Under normal circumstances
you'd play Mortimer the same way that you just played the computerized guy, but since you know he's gapped open you'll take
an entirely different approach. And here we'll have the luxury of
a limit game, which means that Mortimer can't knock us completely out in one hand.

With your hand of Q9, you immediately bet your top pair
after the flop, on-tilt Mortimer raises, you re-raise, Mortimer takes
the third raise, and you cap the betting by using up the fourth.
So you each have a twenty-buck investment before the flop and
fifty dollars each in the pot after the flop, and Fourth Street hasn't
even appeared.

"Jesus Christ," you say, "you're having us bet like morons."

So I might be. But go back to the postulate stating that there
is no bigger sucker in Hold 'Em than the pro or good player
who's on tilt, and add to that the following bit of wisdom: **Never
give a gapped-open player's actions any respect whatsoever
in limit Hold 'Em, even though you'll occasionally lose a
monstrous pot by following this postulate due to the blind-
hog-and-acorn theory. The on-tilt player will raise before just
about every flop regardless of his pocket cards, and will continue to drive the pot like a lunatic after the flop as well.
You should raise this player to the hilt with any legitimate
hand, and even if you lose the occasional pot, in the long
run you'll make considerable hay under these circumstances.
If Mr. On-Tilt continues to fire after Fourth Street appears,**

then you probably should tone your own actions down to merely calling, but as George C. Scott said to Paul Newman in *The Hustler*, stick with this kid because he's a loser. Do not, however, make the mistake of playing recklessly with a third player also in the pot unless your hand is much stronger than the one required to play head-up with the on-tilt guy. (In this example, you could rest assured that if a third player faded all of the raises after the flop, he'd have something better than top pair with a queen kicker—your hand—so you should probably have at least two pair or even better to continue building the pot with a third passenger aboard.) **And don't make the mistake of challenging a gapped-open player unless you have a legitimate hand; you'll often see others calling down an on-tilt player with next to nothing, and those people are playing every bit as poorly as the gapped-open guy. Being on tilt is contagious, and you must learn to hold on to your self-control in a game where other players have lost theirs.**

So much for on-tilt Mortimer. Moving right along, we'll change Mortimer's name to Fred. Let's say you've played with him just as often as you've played with Mortimer. And let's say you know through experience that Fred is a dyed-in-the-wool tightass and when he loses he plays even tighter than normal. Some guys get on tilt when they suffer a few beats, but Fred's someone who is so afraid of being gapped open that he goes too far in the other direction.

Naturally you play Fred differently than you played Mortimer. As for Fred, under normal circumstances, unless you have the nuts or near-nuts, throw your hand away when he bets because Fred thinks a bluff is a rock formation in Montana. But watch his stack. Anytime his chip supply is low, and especially if Fred has to dig in his pocket for more money, that's when it's easy to steal pots from the guy. You're never going to get rich playing against people like Fred, and anytime you sit in a game with seven or eight Freds at the table you should move on to another location as soon as possible. But since a tightass cannot win in Hold 'Em in the long run, you're going to see Fred on the losing end more often than not, and you can take advantage of this situation by bombing a lot of pots—playing aggressively after the flop in order to pick up the pre-flop money. You won't make hay against Fred like you will against a gapped-open Mortimer, but small bombed pots add up to quite a bit in the long run. A word of caution: If, when Fred is loser, he calls your after-the-flop bet, then, unless you're holding the nuts, Fred's got you beat. When that happens, you check when the turn card appears, and when Fred bets behind you, throw your hand away as if the cards were on fire.

We could go on and on with examples of the different player-strategy types you're going to run across, but your opponents' playing habits—be they passive, aggressive, or somewhere in between—are player traits that you'll pick up on as you gain experience in moving from game to game. As we discussed in chapter 4, as a Shark-in-Pigeon's-Clothing you should never play in the same game more than once a week, and since you move around a lot, you'll gain information on a lot of different individuals. As you accumulate and categorize various players and their eccentricities, you're going to be amazed at your brain's storage capacity. And with that bit of sage advice, we're about to close this little exercise, but before we do we're going to give you another postulate: **Ninety-nine out of a hundred poker players behave differently when they are losing than when they are winning, and once you have someone's playing habits committed to memory, the most important indicator you'll have on what to expect from that player is the size of his or her stack of chips. Occasionally you'll run into players who defy this postulate by altering their play so skillfully that putting them on hands is impossible, but those players are the experts who** you're not going to beat in the long run anyway, and who, if you value your bankroll, you should avoid in any sort of head-up confrontation.

If you get nothing more out of this book to improve your poker playing than what's in this chapter, the book will be worth what you pay for it. Remember: **Pay no attention to poker players who babble on and on about tells in people's body language; let these guys go right ahead with their pulled-low hats and sunglasses, and look for them to be chanting ancient apache rhythms while they dance around the campfire in an attempt to bring rain. You develop pattern tells on players by learning their playing habits, and those habits will remain the same no matter what mask the player happens to wear on any given day.**

So there.

11

Money Management

or
If I Run Outta Cash, I Just Go Get Me Some More

The foregoing grammatically deficient yet poignant quote is, word for word, what Johnny Moss once told me after busting out in a game in Midland. Johnny was headed back to Las Vegas by way of Dallas, Dallas being the out-of-the-way stop where he planned to refresh his bankroll. The scene was the clubhouse grill at Tenison Memorial Park Golf Course, and the occasion was Moss dawdling over bacon and eggs as he watched the door for his moneyman to arrive. I sat across from Johnny in a booth, drinking coffee, as I waited for my tee time. Visible through the clubhouse window, Titanic Thompson stroked putt after putt across a bumpy, rock-hard Bermuda practice green.

Johnny Moss's benefactor walked in at nine o'clock sharp, glancing cautiously from side to side as he crossed the room. He slid into the booth alongside the most famous poker player in the world, and handed Moss a paper bag that contained thirty thousand dollars. That doesn't sound like a whole lot of money today, but this was 1965. Moss nonchalantly set the bag up on the table as he continued to chow down on scrambled eggs and burned wheat toast.

The moneyman's name was Dick Martin, a sinewy guy about five and a half feet tall, who among other things was one of the best amateur golfers in America—not to mention that he was also the greatest hustler that the game has ever seen, bar none, including the aforementioned Titanic Thompson who, in the middle-to-late 1960s, ol' Dick used as his personal ATM.

The golf hustler and the poker wizard went back a ways. Once upon a time Moss brought Dick to Las Vegas, then made a small fortune betting on the rail while Dick separated Dean Martin and friends from fifty thousand dollars at the Dunes Country Club. At least, fifty thousand was the sum tossed around between Dino and the Rat Pack over drinks in the Sands lobby lounge, though Dick Martin once told me, cackling, that the real figure was much, much higher.

At the time of the meeting in the Tenison Park grill, both Moss and Martin were in their early fifties and had fared pretty well financially. Moss owned apartment houses in west Texas and some Las Vegas real estate that he'd bought by setting aside some of his poker winnings. Dick Martin, through a lifetime of hustling and living on the cheap while he scrapped for dimes, had accumulated cash in the millions, most of it kept hidden here and there around the city in the form of hundred-dollar bills. While Moss's net worth on paper was substantial, he was, after all, a poker player, and like all poker players he was occasionally strapped for cash. Dick Martin was Johnny Moss's ace in the hole. Show me a no-limit poker player who's been around for a while and, trust me, I'll show you someone who's got a friend like Dick Martin somewhere in the background.

There was and is a code, of course. Dick loved Moss like a brother, but would've lost face if he'd loaned the money interest free, and Moss would never have thought about borrowing without expecting to pay a few points. I never knew the only that Moss got his money for less than the 10 percent week that Martin charged some Dallas bookmakers. The bookies, hopeless gamblers themselves, often needed quick cash to pay their winners while waiting for the losers to come across. Dick died in 1988, and within a couple of years three of Dallas's biggest bookmakers, having lost their ace in the hole, simply weren't around and in business any longer.

Whatever the price of borrowing from Martin, the line of credit was well worth the money to Johnny Moss. Moss often turned the principal into ten times that amount in just a matter of days, and could pay a few thousand in interest without breaking a sweat. He likely could have raised the money in Las Vegas for no interest at all, but there was more at stake in doing that than just getting a loan. Moss didn't want to borrow around Las Vegas because a poker player in need of money loses respect among his peers, and as far as the other players knew, Moss had unlimited funds. When he was broke, Moss just kept his temporary indigence a secret and told the Las Vegas crowd that he was headed home to visit his mother for a few days. Aside from Dick Martin, few were ever the wiser.

Not that Moss always won after Martin had loaned him money. Once Johnny came back four times for more cash before he finally broke out of his losing streak, and during that period I asked Martin if there was a limit to the amount that he'd loan his pal. Ol' Dick seemed deep in thought, but finally laughed and said, "I guess there's a limit, but Johnny ain't gotten there."

I didn't intend for this chapter to evolve into the Dick Martin and Johnny Moss show, but I confess that there's always been a soft spot in my heart for those two, and besides, the Martin and Moss parable is as good a lead-in as any to what I want to cover in the next few pages. This chapter describes the Necessary Poker Bankroll as envisioned by the same people who adhere

ɔd of reading their opponents, versus the
ɔroll as it is in reality. The two are quite dif-
ery poker book on the market gives advice
money required to pay expenses and make
: truth is, however, that no one really knows.
Three .... ɔint: Chris Moneymaker won two and a half
million dollars as the 2003 World Series of Poker Main Event
Champion, Greg Raymer four million a year later, and Joseph
Hachem seven and a half million in 2005. In interviews, each of
those winners said that what they'd won was a life-changing figure. The world assumed that none of these guys would ever have
to worry again about where their next buy-in was coming from.

Oh, really?

Well, if Moneymaker, Raymer, and Hachem had quit playing
high-stakes poker after their World Series wins, the money would
last and last, of course, but telling it like it is, things just don't
work out that way. Once you're established as a Big-Time Poker
Guy, you're expected to act as one, and doing so means that
you'll play regularly upstairs at the Bellagio or some other equally
high-dollar game lousy with the best players in the world. In the
four-and-eight-thousand-dollar limit that goes on daily at the Bellagio, wins and losses amounting to two hundred thousand or
more happen daily, so in an extended losing streak, Chris Moneymaker's prize money would last less than fifteen days, Greg Raymer's
less than thirty, and Joseph Hachem could hold out for just about
a month and a half. If you play poker every day, losing streaks of
a couple of months are as common as dirt no matter the player's
skill level, so a Big-Time Poker Guy's wealth tends to fluctuate.
I wish these three Main Event champions well, but if one or more
 of them shows up penniless in the future—and the rumor around
Las Vegas is that one of them has already done that—I won't be
a bit surprised.

Actual case study: Bill Smith had a serious problem with liquor and died in the late 1980s, but for about thirty years he was known as one of the best no-limit poker players in the world. In 1985 he ascended to the throne, winning the World Series Main Event to the tune of around seven-hundred-thousand. Exactly two weeks to the day after his victory, Smith showed up at a private game in Dallas asking for stake money. (I witnessed this event, and the look on Bill's face as he sat there begging was among the most pitiful sights that I've ever seen.) No one really knows what became of the seven hundred grand in that short period of time, but since Bill spent most of his time running around broke, you have to assume that someone put up his entry fee into the Main Event and that a large chunk of the purse went to whoever that was. The end result was that Bill Smith was indigent one week, won the World Series Main Event in the next, and two weeks after that was back in the same financial shape as before. And Bill Smith's story is by no means an isolated one. In the poker world, Bill Smiths happen every day.

"So okay," you say, "you know all of these here-today-and-gone-tomorrow types, but where in hell are you taking us here?"

Well, maybe nowhere. In fact if you're someone with a steady job, a home, and money in the bank, and poker's just a hobby to you, then other than making you feel really smug that you're in better financial shape than all of these hooked-gambler poker types, this chapter won't be of much benefit. And as far as how to manage your poker money goes, I tend to give all rock-steady homeowners the same advice that they can get from other poker books, and that they can also receive from the hypocritical TV commercial where Harrah's CEO tells you not to gamble when depressed and all that bullshit (as if he really cared). So for our first bit of financial advice, we'll use the common saw handed out to square-john would-be poker players worldwide: Set your spending limit and stick to it, and when that designated sum of money's gone, don't play any more poker until you can once again afford to lose.

But that's advice that you don't really need, isn't it? If you're one of the nose-to-the-grindstone types described above, then you probably limit your poker playing to once-a-week games with "the guys," and you probably aren't reading this book unless you're about to visit Las Vegas with the wife and kids, and think you might sneak away for a few hands of one- and two-dollar limit—unless you can find an even cheaper game. Well, welcome aboard all of you solid suburbanites, but you ain't my prime audience and never will be.

If you are, however, a serious poker player who, at the very least, wants to visit card rooms regularly with the profit motive in mind or, in the extreme, wish to make all or a portion of your living from playing the game, then listen up. We're about to discuss the portion of the Poker Life that's more important than any playing advice you'll ever receive, and even more important than the earlier chapter about where to play and who to be: *staying in money.*

You already know how I feel about playing no-limit, so I won't elaborate except to say that there isn't enough money in the world to sustain a Big-Time Poker Guy through an extended losing streak. So if it's your ambition to bump heads with the big guys, then you'd best establish a relationship with someone you can count on as your ace in the hole. If you've got well-to-do family, that's certainly one avenue for bankroll replenishment, though the decision-makers had better be your mother and dad. (Parents are a good source of whatever you need throughout their lifetimes, but if you're talking an aunt or uncle, or a brother or sister who has a wife or husband with any financial say-so, forget it.) The rules of inter-family finance, as far as one's parents are concerned, are the same with poker players as they are with other prodigals—loan until you can loan no more, don't ever expect repayment, and for God's sake, don't let the other children find out that you're doling it out to the kid who can't keep his or her ass out of the poker parlor.

But if you're one of the 99 percent of us who lack family resources, there are other ways to raise a poker stake. People like Dick Martin, Johnny Moss's ace in the hole, are rare indeed, though they do exist, and if you can find such a person and establish a relationship (the interest will be high, of course, but nothing that you won't be willing to pay), then you'll have a leg up on most of the rest of the poker world. Other poker players can be a source—and a good one, so long as you're willing to reciprocate—but when you run into a situation (and you will someday) where you've got the shorts and your poker-player source is likewise without funds, then you'll have a problem on your hands. I once knew a group of Big-Time Poker Guys who pooled 10 percent of their winnings into a cure fund for the future tapped-outs among them, but that great-in-theory idea went away when one member of the group made off with the pool money and lost it playing craps at the Horseshoe.

So then, the ol' Pigeon's main rule for staying in money as a poker regular will surprise no one who's been paying attention: **Stay away from no-limit poker, or prepare to spend a lifetime hitting on people for loans, acting as an occasional drug mule, plotting speedy in-and-out bank holdups, or some other risk-laden money-raising scheme.**

And you might think that I'm going to advocate skillful limit play as the ultimate answer to the knotty problem of staying in cash, but I'm really not. Sticking to limit games gives you the *best chance* of ducking the broke factor, but limit poker is by no means the alpha and omega of Personal Finance 101 for Gamblers. I could probably list twenty limit players who've survived on their own for many years, but in the Big-Time-Poker-Guy-no-limit category, I can't name a single one who's made it without help of some kind. To clarify, as I've said several times in this book, I'm not acquainted with 100 percent of the TV poker stars, and for all I know some of them might be independently wealthy from their winnings alone. But, you'd be surprised at which high-profile professionals of the ones I do know have to call on their aces in the hole at times to keep on making their games.

So, having described the financial plight of many high-dollar poker players as it is—as opposed to the *public perception* of how it is—I'll now turn my attention to the less high-profile yet more stable folk who inhabit the limit games. And of course, as a limit advocate I'm biased, so I'll begin by using one word to describe the financial outlook for the expert poker players who stick to the limit games.

Bleak.

Oh, very well, *bleak-but-better-than-the-no-limit-guys' outlooks*—but bleak nonetheless. In a short while we'll get into the actual mechanics of staying in money as a poker player, but first a word on attitude. Keeping the proper attitude is the number-one requirement for someone wanting to succeed at this next-to-impossible method of making a living, so I'll begin with another Poker Pigeon's Postulate: **People who attempt to become professional poker players generally fail, not because of inferior play, bad luck, or long negative card runs, but for the same reasons that most small businesses fail, and also for the same reasons that many people retiring from lifelong jobs spend their 401k's in a short period of time and have to go back to work in order to make ends meet. These reasons are, in no particular order: failure to re-invest profits during the good times, irresponsible and out-of-control spending, failure to pre-pare for economic downturn, and general unfamiliarity with short-term prosperity.** Or, more concisely, people who have never had control over large sums tend to spend such money foolishly when they get it and are unable to cope when tough times arrive. Or maybe you've heard it expressed this way: "A fool and his money are soon parted," which is the common man's interpretation of the professorial gobbledegook contained at the beginning of this paragraph.

Sound like the advice your daddy might've given you before turning you loose on society?

One of the least enjoyable parts of the poker life is having to listen to all of the moaning and groaning over bad beats and losing streaks. A great advantage to being counted in with the pigeons of the world is that the poker pro will only pour his heart out to another pro who's going to commiserate and wouldn't dream of complaining to some pigeon who's not in the loop and just wouldn't get it. Absolutely no one is more pitiful than a down-on-his-luck poker player who blames his plight on runs of cards and draw-out beats by pigeons too stupid to fold their hands. Yes, losing streaks exist, and yes, pigeons do draw out with more regularity than the pros like to think about, but if the pigeon never won and the pro never lost, the Poker Life as it is would soon dry up and blow away.

On my last visit to Las Vegas I bumped into a pro who knew me from the old days. This particular guy was floundering in the midst of an unbelievably shitty run of cards, and he told me over lunch at the Horseshoe (I was buying, of course) that what was happening to him was the worst he'd ever seen, and that if things didn't turn around pretty soon he'd have to (horrors) look for a job. I knew beforehand from talking to other players that my dining buddy was on the ropes and that he'd already borrowed from everyone that he knew, used to know, or had happened to bump into in the men's room, so, as I sat there listening, I racked my brain for a gentle way to shortstop the touch that I knew was coming before the meal was over.

When my old buddy said, "Jesus, the rent's due next week," I was pretty sure he was ready to make a play for my wallet, so I said, "Remember the time we went to Monte Carlo?" The trip happened over thirty years ago, but I've never forgotten it and was pretty sure that my friend hadn't either.

He paused in thought, his fork halfway between his plate and his mouth. "The German gal?" he said.

"Right, Krista," I said.

"Jesus, what a set of . . ." He cupped his hands in front of his chest.

"You met her first night there," I said, "after we'd landed in Nice and rented a car. We took her over to Cannes while the festival was going on."

"Yeah, right. Stood next to Doris Day at the crap table. Listen, about this money thing, I was thinking maybe you could—"

"She's the only one I've ever seen," I said, "who was as good-looking in real life as she was up on the screen. Remember, she looked like she wasn't wearing any makeup?"

"You know it's gotta turn around. I could come out of it if I could get my hands on—"

"How much you think you spent on that trip?" I said.

He looked at me.

"We're talking seventies dollars," I said, "but even so. I sat in coach but you were up there where the free liquor flowed, so your round trip ticket had to be, what, seven or eight hundred?"

"Thereabouts. Listen, they got a game at the Mirage so soft you wouldn't believe, and the buy-in's only—"

"I remember I traveled on this package," I said, "got you a few meals and some casino chips, some show tickets for, you know, the package price. You said you'd never be caught dead traveling on one of those packages because you'd never get room service, because they'd think you were a cheapskate and wouldn't tip anything. But hell, I never order room service anyway because it's too expensive. You stayed in this suite and I was on the ground floor rear, so your room was two or three hundred a night, even back then."

He pointed a finger at my chest. "Now, there I've got you. When we checked out I got my room comped, remember?"

"You got your room comped because you blew, what, ten grand at the crap table? I never placed a casino bet, couldn't find a poker game over there, so I kept my cash in my pocket. I remember when we checked out you told the bellhop to be careful not to strain a gut carrying my bags, because I probably had all the towels and ashtrays out of my room stuffed inside. You had some really funny shit to say, you know?"

"Jesus, are you still holding a grudge over that?" he said.

"Hopefully at our age we're beyond grudges," I said. "But you hauled the woman all over Cannes and Monte Carlo, and fed her nothing but the best, crabmeat and lobster, you know, so she had to boost your expenses by at least a grand. When she wanted to know if I'd like to meet her friend, you told her that the friend had better not expect more than a hamburger to eat, maybe a coffee in a drugstore or something. All the while you were making jokes about what a cheapskate I was, old Krista was looking at you like she'd cornered Ross Perot."

"Jesus Christ."

"So all told," I said, "eight hundred for a plane ticket, ten thou at the crap table, another thou to feed the girl and keep her tanked up with liquor, plus I think you bought her a dress or two, which I won't mention, and also I'll keep quiet about the ten-dollar tips you were tossing around to make the girl think you were more hot shit than you really were. Thirteen thousand won't really cover what you spent, but let's call it thirteen, which is eleven thousand more than the trip cost me, plane fare and all."

"I'd made a big win at the time," he said, "twenty grand at the Trop over a ten-day period in the ten-and-twenty game."

"Yeah, you had," I said. "You'd drowned the poker game and thought you deserved a little celebration. But let's say instead of fucking off your money in Monte Carlo, you'd put eleven thousand in an account. In the nineteen seventies, that was when bank interest went up as high as seventeen percent, so conservatively the eleven thousand would be forty today, maybe even fifty."

"I can't cry over spilt milk," he said.

"You're right. You can't," I said, "so tell me why I should have to cry over it when I'm not the one that spilled it. And if you had that forty thousand today, do you think that might get you into a poker game?"

People that knew me years ago would comment that my frugality advice is like the pot calling the kettle black, though I like to equate my little tidbits of wisdom with those of a college professor I once knew. The prof was a strikingly attractive mid-forties woman who taught Marriage and the Family even though she'd been through four divorces. The football players all took Marriage and the Family in order to pull a grade that would keep them eligible, and I was enrolled in the class in order to pull a grade that would keep me from flunking out of school. The prof, who was sleeping with one of the jockstraps in the class, had one ex-husband who taught accounting over in the business school, and one day he called her out so that the two of them could have a knockdown drag-out in the corridor for all of us students to hear. She returned in tears and took a moment to compose herself, then said to the whole class, "Some of you are wondering why I'm teaching this course in light of my own marital problems. So okay, here's the answer in the form of a question: Who knows the pitfalls of marriage better than I do?"

Who indeed?

I was twenty-three years old when I made my first significant poker win, a thousand bucks in a pot-limit game where I started with fifty dollars, and since I'd never had more than a hundred to call my own before, just looking at the stack of Benjamin Franklins on my bed gave me a euphoric dizzy feeling. I drank a bit in those days, so celebrated the big event in a nightclub by ordering a couple of rounds for the house and tossing five-dollar tips around like confetti. The next morning I was down to about seven hundred bucks, and I decided that a newly rich man such as I could use a set of wheels. So I went to a we-tote-the-note car lot and drove away in an awesome black '57 Chevy with a red interior for two hundred down. In twenty-four hours I'd spent half of my winnings, so I decided to return to the poker game to replenish my bankroll, and naturally I lost the $500 I had left in less than an hour. Seven days later my Chevy went away like my cash, repossessed when I couldn't meet the weekly payment. As the tow truck hauled my beautiful car around the corner, I decided that the thousand-dollar win hadn't done me all that much good.

Another time I was out of money but did have a Visa with cash advance privileges, so I borrowed fifteen hundred dollars on the credit card (at something like 30 percent apr) to get into a poker game where I won three thousand dollars. Instead of re-paying my cash advance I went on a department store spending spree, ended up with a *GQ*-level wardrobe, and of course lost the rest of my money a day later in the same poker game where I'd won the three thousand. Thirty days later my Visa got cancelled.

Who knows the pitfalls better than I do?

No one. If there is a foolish way to spend poker winnings, I've done it numerous times.

But hey, I now have money stashed and read the Tightwad's Gazette religiously. Honest Injun, fellas, I've changed.

And you old-guys-that-knew-me-when can say "Yeah, sure" as loud as you want to, but nothing will render the advice I'm about to give any less valid. There is no profession where the temptation to spend money foolishly is stronger than that of a professional poker player, and wasting money is the number-one reason that very few professional poker players stay around very long.

The successful pros I know have one thing in common: All have learned to *give the impression* of being loose with the dollar while in truth they're just the opposite. They stay at the best casino hotels, but always at a special rate, and eat lunch in first-class restaurants, but always with a sharp eye for the nooner specials. If you invite one of them to dinner on your nickel, well and good, and you'd better take plenty of money along to pay the tab, but if there is any chance that it's a Dutch-treat proposition, he or she will always decline; and if you shadow these poker pros after they've declined your dinner invitation, you'll be likely to find them chowing down in some greasy spoon or fast-food emporium. Aside from hanging on to their money until George Washington squints in the glare every time they bring a dollar into the open, there is another method in the madness of pretending to spend it when really they're not. The poker lightweights whose pockets the pros are picking are for the most part uncontrollable spendthrifts, and the pros don't want to give the idea that they're anything other than one of the gang. I once knew a pro who got into a money-tossing contest, where he and his special pigeon took turns wadding up ten-dollar bills and throwing them into a wastebasket to demonstrate their lack of regard for money. The next morning I found the pro waist deep in garbage, standing upright in the Dumpster behind the building, retrieving every ten-dollar bill that he could lay his hands on.

Another pitfall to the poker life: Too many self-conceived poker professionals are in fact hopeless gamblers, and poker is just one of the many outlets they use for flushing their money down the drain. I haven't played a hand of blackjack or put money on the line at the crap table in over twenty years, and I doubt that I've put a total of five dollars in slot machines in my entire life. I don't know the rules to Pai Gow, Caribbean Stud, or Baccarat, and have no desire to learn them. Since card rooms are nearly all run in conjunction with casinos, bad proposition gambles are on all sides of poker players twenty-four hours a day, and if craps and blackjack don't do the trick of separating the would-be Brunsons of the world from their winnings, there are always the sports books. Bookies play in just about every poker game in the world these days, taking sports bets right at the table, and the bookie is always too busy writing the action down to be much of a factor in the poker game. In Nevada, the legal sports book is located just across the casino floor from the card room.

I've never seen a compulsive gambler succeed in the long run as a poker pro, and if you're determined to try to profit from your poker skills, you simply must never bet on anything other than poker. ESPN makes great sport during the World Series of all the wild bets made among the regular Las Vegas players— there was one guy who even received *breast implants* to win a bet, for Christ's sake—but no matter how famous the poker player happens to be or how much of a star the TV folks attempt to make of him, if he's wagering ten grand on something like which bird flies off of a tree first, that person has a serious problem, and you can rest assured that he's not going to stay in money for very long. And if you're one of the many who can't keep the blinders on and your eyes on the prize instead of the football scores, then you should avoid poker rooms like the plague, because one of the truest clichés in the English language is that one thing leads to another, and anyone with a gambling problem should stick to being an accountant or bartender or whatever else they're able to do for a living. Successful poker players are by no means gamblers, never have been, and never will be.

I'll now dispense with the tree-stump breast-beating about money wasting in general. You've no doubt received enough frugality advice to last you a lifetime, so we'll now turn to a discussion of what you really want to know—the size of the bankroll required for you to have a legitimate shot at poker riches, and how much you should put at risk in each session at the poker table. Formula with a capital *F*, right? Well, you've come to the right place, kids, and who should know more on this subject than an old-time smart-money poker hustler such as your truly? Nobody, that's who, and my answer to these burning questions is . . .

Is . . .

That I don't have the slightest fucking idea.

If you're a beginner or a really shitty veteran player trying to get better and you have to go through an improvement period before you can begin your assault on the poker world, then you're naturally going to need more money than an expert player who decides to turn pro à la Tiger Woods, who was already the best golfer in the world before he ever stuck a tee in the ground with money on the line. I've read a poker book that says you should have a thousand times the limit for whatever game you're playing, in order to give the percentages plenty of time in which to take hold (twenty grand to play ten-and-twenty dollar limit, in other words), and I've read another poker book stating that you should never risk more than ten percent of your bankroll in any one session. Sage advice, what?

Well, I beg to differ. I know a guy who was the superintendent of schools in a rural Texas community before he became a full-time poker professional. Though he'd grown up around poker games and his father was a high-dollar gambler known in Las Vegas and points west, my buddy had promised his mama that he'd stay on the straight and narrow. By the time he was thirty years old he'd earned a master's in education and a solid status in the community. He also had a home with astronomical mortgage payments, around twenty dollars in the bank, and was up to his ass in debt to the credit card companies. One payday he scraped together two hundred bucks and headed for the nearest poker game, and a year later was completely debt free and had a pile of hundred-dollar bills tucked away. Tongues wag in small towns, of course, and my friend got word that if he was to continue as school superintendent, he'd have to cool it with the gambling life, so he thumbed his nose at the education system and struck out on the poker circuit. That was over thirty years ago and this guy has never looked back. So his necessary poker bankroll was two hundred bucks. Go figure.

I know another guy who started with thirty thousand dollars, lost that, lost two more thirty-thousand-dollar grubstakes, finally turned things around, and over the past fifteen years has won, conservatively, three million dollars at the poker table. So this man's necessary poker bankroll was about ninety grand. Go figure that one as well.

And I knew another guy . . .

Oh, hell—you get the idea. We're talking about a game where, if you play it well, you'll come out fabulously in the long run, but anyone who tells you that they can predict *how long* it will take for you to come out ahead is pulling your chain.

I confess that it's been a few years since I've had to worry about a poker bankroll, but back when I was less affluent than I am, here's what I used to do: I never worried about long-term play. I just wanted enough money to buy into a game once, and if I won that day I'd play again the next day, and I'd keep on playing as long as I could live on my winnings and still keep buy-in money. On the other hand, if I bought in that first time and lost, then I didn't play again until I'd gone back to work and earned enough money for another buy-in. I was never a good employee because I'd wanted a career playing poker since Day One out of college, so I wasn't interested in whatever job I held at any particular time over the long haul. For about fifteen years I followed the same pattern: accumulate a bankroll, play poker, and if I won keep on playing until I needed another bankroll, then look for a job that would furnish enough to put me back in action in as short a time as possible. I recently checked my records with the government and was surprised to learn that I had enough quarters under social security to qualify, so I think I'll start in drawing benefits when I'm seventy if I make it that long. Jesus, I can drag down over fifteen hundred a month then, and that should be plenty to buy into any reasonable limit game.

Many poker players are excellent dealers, though they aren't interested in a career dealing poker and will only work in a card room as long as it takes to raise a playing bankroll. Poker rooms understand these players' wants and always have spots on the payroll with player sustenance in mind. A friend of mine has lived in Las Vegas for thirty years and estimates that he's dealt in card rooms for a third of the time and spent the other twenty years living off his poker winnings. He has a good reputation among card room managers, so whenever he goes broke he can get a job the following day.

There is one last point that needs making before I draw this lesson to a close, and that has to do with how long one should spend at the table on any given day. I've read books by poker pros who say that the only issues that determine when to quit are the skill of the other players in the game and other obligations that you can't get out of. Your length of play, the pro goes on, should never depend on the time of day or whether or not you're winning; if the game's really good, you should stay as long as the pigeons will keep on fogging the money in. This theory sounds right the first time you hear it: the pro is saying that if you're a superior player and never get rattled, you hold the advantage in the long run and therefore should never quit unless you have to. But on close examination the pro is all wet. Here's why.

The poker player who can keep his or her cool whatever the circumstance simply doesn't exist, and if you sit there long enough, fatigue will set in and your game will suffer. There is no one alive who doesn't go on tilt after a series of horrendous beats, and playing while exhausted and on tilt will send you to the poorhouse in a hurry. How long one can sit upright and maintain concentration, and the number of beats that must occur before one goes on edge depends on the player. I know folks who can play at a high level for days on end, and I know players who lose their concentration after only a few hours, and if you want to enter this life or any portion of it, you must set your own limits and stick to them. The whiner/loser poker pros claim that their skill level remains high, but watch their actions closely and you'll see that that claim has no validity—the longer they play the worse they play, and if they sit there long enough, their bankroll will go completely in the toilet.

My own m.o. is to restrict my playing time to five hours per session, after which I quit no matter what the results, and also to curb my daily losses at thirty times the upper limit in the game—nine hundred dollars playing fifteen-and-thirty, six hundred dollars playing ten-and-twenty, etc. When my time is up, I quit. When my losses reach the designated amount, I quit as well. I refuse to get unrecoverably stuck in any game or to swim upstream against the current on and on into the night, and I believe that poker players who allow themselves to get drowned in any one sitting have no chance whatsoever to come out ahead in the long run. Other than those two little playing rules, coupled with controlling my spending away from the poker table, there is little else to my secret, and I've survived for many more years than the norm.

I'm sorry if this chapter has painted a less-than-rosy picture of the poker player's life, but I think I'd be remiss if I didn't level with you. If you aspire to be a pro, or to earn any portion of your living from playing poker, then skillful play certainly helps and so does the ability to read your opponents based on your experience in playing with them. But hear this: **If you have a** gambling problem that you can't control or you can't keep from blowing your money right after a big win, then you're better off with a job where your employer puts you in a solid 401k and doles out your income on a monthly basis. Inability to manage income is certain death to a poker player. If you're unable to keep up with your money, then trying to play poker to create income is going to be a waste of time no matter how skillful a player you become.

12

On Grabbing A Seat In Cyberspace

or

Your Money? You're Worried About Your Money?? Just Keep on Playin', Pal, and We'll Send Your Money Later—What the Hell Are You Worried About? Ain't You Seen Our Ad on ESPN???

I've heard that there are ten times as many people who play poker over the Internet as there are flesh and blood, real-live poker players, and I wouldn't be surprised if the true figure is even higher. I've heard guys on television say that the Internet is the main creation responsible for the nationwide poker explosion and that cyberspace play has caused a sharp increase in the number of qualified poker experts walking around. Internet tournament winners occupied over half of the seats at the '05 World Series of Poker (in case you missed them, they were the guys who, accustomed to playing in secret where no one can see how stupid they look, danced around like lunatics every time they won a pot). I golf some with a guy who won four thousand dollars in an Internet tournament where he bought in for something like fifty dollars, and this guy swears that online is the safest place to play that there is.

Oooo-kay. So here are my conclusions: (1) Online poker play is great for online poker rooms. (2) Online poker play is great for the people running the World Series of Poker because of the added house rake created by 5600 entrants where there used to be 50.

I'll sum up my feelings regarding Internet play in general with another anecdote: In a lifetime of playing I've been in three games where I know that a "cold deck" came into play (this is a method of cheating where the deck is pre-stacked, and where one of the players besides the deck stacker must be in on the scam in order to perform the ol' false cut). That's not to say that I haven't played in other games where I *suspected* cheating, but the three games I'm talking about are the only ones where I *absolutely know* that my pocket got picked because the players in on the scams later bared their souls.

The people involved in running the crooked poker games were (1) a notorious old gambling cheat, (2) a lawyer (who else?), and (3) a good-looking woman who dazzled you with charm while she ran up the deck on you. The old cheat died a few years back. The crooked lawyer and the crooked babe got so well known in the gambling community that they had to leave the country. As of two years ago, the lawyer was in Belize and the babe was in Aruba.

Both were running online poker rooms.

'Nuff said? It oughtta be, but in case I'm not getting my point across, there's more.

Online gambling got big in the mid 1990s, first with sports books and standard casino games, such as craps, blackjack, and cyberspace slot machines. Internet casinos began to add poker in, oh, 1996 or 1997, and today there are numerous websites that function as poker rooms only, exclusive of the other casino operations. And, yeah, I know the standard saws such as, *they've got no need to cheat when they've got the odds going for them, and as for the poker, they're just operating on the rake anyway so why do they care who wins?* If you're one of the millions subscribing to that policy, listen up to the following:

A friend came to me about eight years ago. He didn't play

poker but loved the casino games, and he'd begun to play a little online blackjack at a casino website that featured different tables with different limits and rules—Vegas Strip, Downtown Vegas,
and Atlantic City Trump rules, as I remember, the difference in
local rules having to do with what two-card combinations the
player can double down with (in some casinos it's ten or eleven
only, in others players can double with any two cards), and whether
the player can double down at any time or can double down only
after the first two cards are dealt. The most liberal blackjack rules
happen in Atlantic City, so my friend was playing Atlantic City
Trump, two hands at once at twenty bucks apiece, when a little
glitch in the action occurred.

The dealer's upcard was a ten-count (either a ten or a face
card, I don't remember which) and my buddy had two aces in
one of his hands and two eights in the other. Following good
basic strategy, my friend split both hands. On his two aces he
caught a nine and a face for one total of 20 and another total
of 21. On his eights he caught a deuce and a trey for 10 and
11, and on doubling both of these hands he caught another ace
on one and a facecard on the other, for a pair of 21s. So he now
had a total of $120 in bets down, and held one 20 and three
21s against the dealer's ten-count upcard. Great for the player,
right? Well, guess again.

The dealer exposed his downcard, which turned out to be an
ace for a natural 21—blackjack. The damfool online dealer then
scooped up my friend's bets and toted them all away.

Say what?

Right. The dealer's natural blackjack beat all four of my buddy's
hands, at least according to that particular casino. The problem
was this: The dealer wasn't playing by Atlantic City Trump rules,
as advertised, or by any other legitimate American blackjack rules
that anyone I've ever spoken to is aware of. It's true that natural
21 beats all other hands, but in this case the casino *allowed my friend*

to play his hands out, doubling his bets until he had one hundred twenty dollars on the table instead of his original twenty, when my friend had already lost when the first two-card hands had come off of the deck! The house won as it was supposed to, but the natural blackjack should have been revealed as soon as it was dealt, and my friend should have only lost forty dollars instead of the one hundred and twenty dollars that the online casino took from him.

That's cheating, folks, pure and simple. My friend asked me what he should do.

And, man, was I ever a crusader for the public good. This guy had come to me to right a wrong because in his mind I was the gambling expert (okay, he wasn't much of a gambler himself and didn't know poker from blackjack), so I used my buddy's e-mail address to fire off a hot message to the online casino demanding that he get an eighty-dollar refund. The casino ignored this e-mail, so three days later I sent an even nastier e-mail, this time stating that if they didn't refund my friend's eighty dollars I was going to turn them in to the online gambling police (which didn't and don't exist, of course, but I was hoping that the casino guys didn't know that). And when *that* message got no response, I wrote another nasty e-mail for my buddy to send these online pirates *every day.* Two weeks later my friend called to tell me he'd finally heard back from the online casino. I dropped everything, hauled ass over to my friend's place with bated breath, and looked at the message from the casino written in bold strokes across my buddy's computer monitor.

The message contained two words. It said: BUZZ OFF.

Really, that's what it said.

Now I *really* got on my high horse. Back in those days people gambled over the Internet using a credit card (which they can no longer do, but more on that in a moment), so I told my pal to contact his credit card company and have all charges to that casino reversed. He did so. Two weeks later he called me again, because the casino had sent two collection goons out to his home. I rushed over to his place as a protector, but believe me, my attitude quickly changed once I arrived. I mean, these two guys were *goons*! The end result was that my buddy forked over, in cash, and hopefully learned his lesson.

About now you're saying to yourself, *So what does this have to do with all of these online poker rooms that make their money from raking pots and therefore have no incentive to cheat?*

Well, it has *this* to do with it: Just about a year and a half after the above incident, my friend called me over to show me a bulk e-mail he'd received, wherein this *same casino* had now opened an online poker room and was offering deposit bonuses, etc., etc., etc., if my friend would come play poker at their comfortable, secure, really cool website. My friend declined. He still doesn't play poker, and as far as I know, to this day he's never placed another bet over the Internet. He still plays casino craps and blackjack, but at least he does it in person.

And, oh, yeah, as long as we're talking incentives to cheat . . .

Let's suppose that you own one of these online poker rooms, and let's suppose that you aren't the George Washington, never-tell-a-lie, I-chopped-down-the-cherry-tree type of individual that I know you are. And let's suppose that you want to make as much money as you possibly can from your website, and that you think you deserve more than the three or four bucks a pot that you're currently knocking down. How would you do it?

Increase your rake?

That's certainly one way to bulk up profits, and since no government authority regulates your operation, you can rake whatever in hell you want to. But if you do up your rake, you'll lose a lot of business. There are ten million competing Internet gambling joints, and each one keeps a close eye on all of the others, and it wouldn't be forty-eight hours after you raised your take that the bulk e-mails would go out all over the world, stating that

you are an overcharging creep and that everyone should desert
your crooked poker joint and come over to the bulk e-mailer's
crooked poker joint. So discard upping your rake as a bad idea.

So what's a better idea?

Well, why not keep it all? Why not put every dime deposited
on your website in your own pocket, which would increase your
current rake by a thousand percent or more?

"No way could I do that," you say. "Then there would be no
winners on my site, and everyone would quit playing with me
and go elsewhere."

Come on. This is the ol' Poker Pigeon you're talking to.

Remember I said a page or so back that we'd further discuss
credit cards as a deposit method on Internet gambling websites?
Okay, the coast is clear and now's the time, and before you ac-
cuse me of wandering far afield from my subject matter, please
believe that I'll tie credit card deposits into my discussion of online poker in just a little bit. Back when online gambling was in
its infancy, Visa and Master Card were the primary deposit methods, and the credit card companies loved the business that computer gambling created. Any gambling deposit made with a credit
card was treated as a cash advance, which meant a higher interest rate and an origination fee, and for a number of years the
online casinos and credit card companies walked hand in hand
down the garden path, strewing rose petals in their wake. But in
the late '90s that all changed, and today any request for online
deposits gets a quick rejection from Visa, MasterCard, or whatever other bank card you're trying to use. Today, in fact, making online casino/poker room deposits are the biggest pain in
the ass involved in the entire process of playing over the Internet—not that wire transfers and bank wires and whatnot have
slowed down the online action; just the opposite, there are now
more folks playing in cyberspace than there ever were.

So why no more credit card deposits? Did the bank/credit

card companies suddenly realize that Internet gambling might be illegal in this country and show their support for America by refusing to do business with these thieves who lived in foreign countries?

Not on your life, kids. Banks are just as greedy as they ever were, and the sudden stoppage of credit card companies from accepting charges from gambling websites has nothing to do with banks' concern with U.S. law or their customers' welfare or any of the other garbage they'd like to blow up your skirts. The credit card companies stopped doing business with online casinos because of a California class-action lawsuit that a woman filed against several of the majors. This woman alleged that the credit card company conspired with the online casino to bilk her out of hundreds of thousands of dollars, and that since her six-figure balances with the credit card companies consisted of gambling debts, which are uncollectible under U.S. law, she didn't have to pay the credit card companies *nada*. The courts agreed with her to the tune of a six-figure forgiven debt and a couple of million in punitive damages. So much for casino deposits made by credit card.

Today, online casinos and poker operations spend a high percentage of their time in figuring out how to get money from U.S. pockets into theirs. Western Union used to be a casino conspirator, but U.S. law enforcement has closed that avenue by threatening prosecution of Western Union for violation of U.S. gambling laws. Then the casinos set up a deal with something called NeTeller.com, which opened nationwide accounts in U.S. banks, where the suckers could make direct bank deposits using NeTeller's account numbers, but the feds eventually closed *that* loophole by threatening the banks with conspiracy charges the same as they'd done to Western Union. Currently the offshore gambling operations have a new wrinkle, one where the mark can use his credit card to buy minutes on a *long-distance phone card,* for Christ's sake, and then have those funds somehow transferred into online casino coffers as deposits. I suspect that even the credit card companies are ignorant of the phone card companies' involvement in gambling over the Internet, though they must be curious about why so many of their customers make thousands of dollars' worth of long-distance phone calls when they could use cell phone plans with free weekend minutes and all of that bullshit, and save the long-distance money. I suspect the feds will figure out a way to short-circuit the phone card scam eventually, but then the online casinos will come up with something new to circumvent even *that* closed loophole. The one-upmanship game between the feds and the online gambling operations goes on and on.

So what's my point, or at least the point I'm trying to make in connection with online poker rooms? Well, for one thing, rumor has it that the woman who was the plaintiff against the credit card companies eventually lost all of her lawsuit proceeds back to the *same casinos to whom she'd given the six-figure credit card deposits,* and if the rumors are true, then the bad guys got the money in the long run and the middleman/credit card company got the bag to hold. And this lady wasn't atypical by any means; in spite of all the hoopla about the convenience of playing from your own home, online gamblers are for the most part compulsives who use the Internet as a tool for gambling in secret. Just think about it. Why would anyone lay down his or her money over the Internet to people they don't know—and have no way of investigating—when they could make a short-to-medium drive, walk into a casino and play, and, if they were lucky enough to win, carry their winnings over to the cage and walk out with cash in their pockets.

So anyway, your presumption that if there were no winners on your website, people would all quit playing with you, is dead wrong. If you set up every poker game so that the live one was actually playing against nine computer characters and the bots always won, then your website could keep 100 percent of the money deposited, and since none of these compulsive online gamblers would confide in others that they were playing and losing every day, you wouldn't lose a nickel's worth of business.

There's a common practice among these online establishments that in my mind, more than anything else they do makes them suspect: that's their payout practice whenever the sucker does happen to win. Every one of the cyberspace casinos or poker rooms has a deposit method—be it bank wire, wire transfer, phone card purchase, or whatever—that transfers your money into their hands *right fucking now*, but when the cash is going in the other direction the story is completely different. Please explain why, when the casino or poker room can take money out of your bank account instantaneously, it can't pay your winnings off in exactly the same way. It can, of course, but it chooses not to. When you cash in you'll get a message that your money will be transferred within twenty-four hours (and believe me, you won't get it one second before that), and if you want to keep playing in the meantime, the casino will simply deduct what you lose from whatever amount they're paying you. The casino's plan is, naturally, that by the time they have to come across you won't have any more money due.

The online payout practice makes perfectly good sense in an operation where the sucker is playing against the house—they're hoping you'll keep playing and donate your winnings back to them, of course—but if an online poker parlor is operating strictly off of its rake and has games going 24/7, why should the poker operation care who wins or who loses or when they get paid? Well, the poker room shouldn't care, *unless* you are in fact playing against a bunch of its robots and the poker room wants to hold your money for the same reason that the blackjack and craps operators don't want to pay you—in hopes that you'll keep on playing until you have nothing left to cash in.

This chapter is likely going to create some controversy once this book is published, so since I'm an up-front and in-your-face kind of guy, I'll deal right here and now with an argument you're going to hear in the online casinos' favor. *"If these online casinos are cheating,"* some online players are going to say, *"then how come every year a bunch of their customers show up to play in the World Series, buy-ins in hand? If the Internet places were dishonest, wouldn't they also pit tournament players against a bunch of robots so they could keep 100 percent of the tournament entry fees as well?"*

Why, hell, no. Dishonest or not, Internet card room operators certainly aren't dumb. World Series of Poker time is when online card rooms get their prime exposure, their ads before the public, and their tournament winners right there on television for the entire world to see. As you're going to see in the next chapter, tournament play is the most profitable item for casinos that there is, percentage-wise, and the odds of the players winning are many times worse than the odds against them in any casino game where they're playing against the house. Therefore you may rest assured that Internet tournament play is totally Honest Injun, because it is to the online poker rooms' advantage to keep the tournaments fair and square, and while entering a tournament is the worst gamble that a player can come across, the player can rest assured that the game's going to be on the up-and-up. But when it comes to cash games held in cyberspace, both the incentive and the opportunity for the house to cheat increase dramatically.

So wait a minute. Am I saying that all Internet play, other than tournament competition, is crooked, and that when playing over the Internet a player absolutely cannot win?

No, I'm not saying that at all; I'm only pointing out the dangers of online play if the card room operators *were of a mind* to cheat. And in fact, the potential cheating devices, such as the employment of bots, aren't used 100 percent of the time. Of that

I am certain. What I personally believe is that cheating occurs in cash games over the Internet *about half* the time, and that when you sit down at a cyberspace table set for ten, about five of the players will be fictional computer-generated characters and about four of your opponents will be suckers, the same as you. So, yeah, you can win, though your chances of winning in cyberspace are cut in half compared with your chances in a live casino. I do believe that if you play on the Internet over an extended period of time, you're going to lose in the long run no matter how skillful your play. Online casinos and card rooms are totally unregulated in this country, and while they probably do hold casino licenses in whatever country they call home (though it's not a cinch that they do), if they cheat you over the Internet, the only law they're going to violate is U.S. law. They break local, state, and federal statutes—and you do as well—the second that you log in and start to play, so what additional risk are they running by cheating? None. U.S. law enforcement has proven to be helpless against these online gambling sites. Whatever happens to you in cyberspace stays in cyberspace, and you can expect no help whatsoever from the police or FBI if the online poker rooms cheat you.

I guess you could call my attitude toward Internet poker another case of sour grapes on my part, and I'll admit that much of the animosity I feel is the result of my experience playing in cyberspace. Here's the story in a nutshell: About five years ago in New York City—as a matter of fact, in the underground poker joint that (according to the game runners, anyway) served as a model for the poker club identified in the movie *Rounders* as the Chesterfield—a guy told me about an online poker room where he played most days and where he was winning so much money that he was thinking about retiring from live games altogether. As soon as I got home I checked on the website, downloaded its software, and got ready for a career knocking 'em dead in cyberspace. I remember distinctly telling my wife, "Gee, honey, I think I can pick up a grand a week or more sitting in my own house, and this may be such a good deal that I'll never again have to hit the road." I tested the water by depositing five hundred dollars in my card room account, and by mucking around for starters in the two-and-four and three-and-six-dollar limit games.

Thank God I started out small.

At a hundred bucks a pop, I lost my buy-in to small-limit on-line Hold 'Em games *twenty-six times in succession*. Over the past forty years I've played in games with people reputed to be the best in the world, in riverboat games, European games, games in thirty-seven U.S. states, you name it, and *I have never lost over five times in a row in any game I've ever played in*. I have observed all sorts of winning and losing streaks in my life, and *I have never seen the world's biggest sucker—and I'm not about to call that guy by name—lose in any limit Hold 'Em game twenty-six times in a row*.

And what do my consecutive losses in Internet poker prove? If your guess is "nothing," you're right, of course. (Critics of this book are going to say that my consecutive losses prove that I'm a crappy poker player, but I swear on the Bible that I'm really not.) Cards have no memory, and it is statistically possible for any poker player, regardless of skill, to lose in every game he or she plays in for the rest of his or her life. But consider this: *Not only did I lose twenty-six consecutive times, I was never ahead in any of those games—not even once*. And I agree with what you're thinking, that if the games weren't on the up-and-up, then the operators should have let me win a time or two in order to fatten me up for the kill. That never happened, and the fact that I never was ahead gave me the incentive to keep on trying. The game must be on the square, I thought, because a crook would let me rake a pot or two in order to make it look good. And as

I write this I *still* think that an online cheat should let the sucker win occasionally, but that doesn't recover my money, does it?

Since there's no way to prove online cheating, especially with no regulatory authority looking over the game operators' shoulders, let me interject something else about Internet play that I found weird. In a lifetime of playing Hold 'Em in live games I've seen a "set over a set over a set" (three players holding pocket pairs all catching trips on the flop) exactly once, and the incident was so rare that I remember the exact location, date, and even the time, within fifteen minutes either way (Great Southwest Golf Club, Grand Prairie, Texas, June 9, 1983, sometime between eight-thirty and nine o'clock in the evening—and the guys in the game, if they read this, will now know who's writing this book, but I can't help that) and can even tell you what the three sets were (nines, sixes, and deuces). Playing over the Internet, however, I saw a set over a set over a set *three times during one playing session.*

Is it possible that the three different incidents of set over set over set in online play was a mere coincidence? Sure it is, but . . .

In the same number of years playing Hold 'Em as outlined above, I have seen "quads over quads" (two players holding four of a kind) a few times, but very rarely, and in card rooms offering Bad Beat Jackpots, the losing quads generally take home the five-figure prize. I saw quads over quads in Internet poker *six times in one four-hour session.*

So is it also possible that the six instances of quads over quads is a coincidence? Sure it is, but even a mule reacts if socked between the eyes with a hammer often enough. After six solid months witnessing such coincidences over and over and over again, I was like Roberto Duran—*no más, no más, no más.* And, as if I didn't have enough incentive to quit all Internet play, try the following on for size: *After absorbing beating after beating over the Internet, I learned, purely by accident, that the guy who'd tipped me off*

to the website was also part owner of the online poker operation,
something that he of course neglected to tell me.

But let's change gears for a moment and quit the Internet
poker room bashing. Let's assume that I'm full of it, and that in
truth every single online poker operation is honest, so honest
that the Internet card room operators have staff meetings every
day where they agonize for hours over how to give the online
player a fairer and squarer deal. Let's assume, in fact, that there
is an Online Poker Police Department, that every online poker
room operator has to wear an electronic device around his nuts,
and that every time an operator cheats, the device squeezes his
balls and puts him on his knees.

Know what? I still don't wanna play.

When I decided to try online poker, I abandoned some of the
cardinal rules I'd set for myself. I was playing in a game where
I couldn't identify the performers (Analytical Man, Desperate
Man, etc.), where I couldn't quit and collect my money on my
way out, and, most critical, where any pigeon moves I made
would most likely go undetected among the other players in the
game. I mean, really—if I didn't know the identity of Breasty
Susan, Ucum2lose, Vegas Vic, and whatever other user names sat
around the table (or, indeed, if any of these people actually existed outside of cyberspace), and if the website was telling the
truth when it said that four jillion thousand players were currently in action in the poker joint, then how in hell could I possibly keep up with all these folks and their playing habits, and
how in hell could any of them possibly notice when I put the
Weak Player's Fourth-Street Check-Raise into play? I couldn't.
They couldn't. The only sensible strategy for playing online poker
was to revert to Sklansky and hope for the best, and since any
knowledgeable players among my opponents would also be playing by Sklansky's rules, and since I couldn't possibly identify the
weak players going in because of my lack of experience in play-

ing with them, then online play would become a game of Racehorse, or First-One-Over-Wins. I refuse to play Racehorse with
anyone; therefore, other than my 0-for-26 half-year Internet experiment, I've refrained from online play and always will.

(I should mention here that online poker addicts will take issue
with the preceding paragraph, and will maintain that they keep
intricate notes on their opponents' playing habits and can therefore read everyone at the table like a book. My only response is
that I believe anyone claiming to keep up with the individual
playing habits of thousands of Internet players is either (1) lying—
and actually losing their ass playing over the Internet—or (2) a
person of such enormous brain capacity that they should be locked
away, where the same herd of shrinks that studied John Nash for
years could have a go at them. Besides, even if you could keep
up with thousands of individuals and their screen names and playing habits, how do you know that Ucum2lose sitting across from
you now is the same Ucum2lose that sat across from you last
month, or if maybe Ucum2lose has run in a ringer to play in his
place, or even—worst case—if Ucum2lose is in fact a bot that
the poker room operators have programmed to play differently
than the last time you saw him, and who is also programmed to
hold the nuts every time you play in a pot with him? You can't
know, and therefore I maintain that you shouldn't play.)

The ol' Poker Pigeon's take on online poker play is drawing
to a close, but I do want to leave you with one more scenario to
consider. The assumptions here are, once again, that the Internet game is all on the up-and-up and that you have a mind that's
the Microsoft main frame's envy and are therefore hip to each of
your thousands of opponents' playing habits and a heavy favorite
to win. So here's a way I can screw you anyhow. Suppose I'm
in cahoots with two buddies, and that my two buddies and I are
located in different places with computers in front of us and that
we are all logged on to the same website and, by going through

the Wait List process, have all gotten seats in the same poker game. Suppose that while playing, each of us has two cell phones to keep us in constant contact with the other two guys. Why, all we have to do is tell each other what our pocket cards are so that when one of us holds the nuts the other two can raise it up like gangbusters, and you and the rest of the players in the game are dead meat. And that, kids, is the easiest way for the players—forget the house and its opportunities to pull fast ones for a moment—to cheat in Internet poker, and is also a method that the online operators would be powerless to stop even if, for God's sake, the freaking *Pope* were running the game.

So now I'm through with the online games and, as always, your bucks are your bucks, and you're free to spend them any way that you choose. But as for me, if I'm playing poker with anyone, I'm going to be looking at them, and I'm never again falling for the line that the road to poker riches is only a click away.

13

In the Company of the Big Boys

or

If That's Ol' Doyle Across the Table, Then I Must Have Finally Arrived, Baby

Stop yawning. This is the final chapter, and it's also the one that the don't-get-its among you have been waiting for. This is the one where we're throwing caution to the wind, climbing those steps to the summit, wading right on in there with the Doyles, Howards, Annies, Daniel Negreanus, and Chip Reeses of the world, and where we're going to . . . going to . . .

Well, the truth is that we're probably going to lose our asses, but remember, you asked for it, and we're here to please. This ain't the kiddie game. This is no-limit, where they separate the men from the boys. (Or is it where the rubber meets the road? Whatever . . .)

This is now officially a serious matter, so let's get serious. Even though I've told you over and over to steer clear of no-limit poker, you wouldn't listen, so I'm going to give you some hints as to the best way to play no-limit if you're determined to. Expect this chapter to be concise and to the point. If you win, great. If you lose, don't blame me.

We'll start with cash game no-limit and then move on to tournament play. The two are quite, quite different because of the sharp contrast in player goals. In a cash game your objective is to win as much as possible from whomever possible, and short-term losses don't mean all that much because you can always buy more chips. In a freeze-out tournament your goal is to survive while other players knock each other out in the early going, and experienced tournament warriors (1) steer clear of players with bigger chip stacks than theirs until the tournament reaches its final stage so that they can (2) become more and more aggressive as the process of elimination narrows the field. You make calls and run bluffs in cash games that you'd never dream of in a tournament and vice versa.

So, moving right along, here we go with the Poker Pigeon's No-Limit Cash Game Postulate #1: **A common mistake in no-limit Hold 'Em is to go in on short money and hope to win big. While cheap buy-ins will occasionally grow into small fortunes playing no-limit, the player with the most chips in front of him has a tremendous advantage over the field and in nearly all instances will knock out the short buys before they can get any sort of foothold—and having the most chips at all times, folks, more than any skillful play or tricky maneuvering, is the reason that you'll see the same no-limit players winning over and over. These people simply don't play unless they're in a position to scare up a bankroll and put a pile of chips in front of them the size of Philadelphia. The bigger the difference between the fattest player's stack and the second-fattest guy's, the more advantage that big fatty has. If you have five hundred dollars and big fatty has five thousand, then you have to go all-in with big fatty and beat him at least twice in a row to have any chance at all.**

And on the heels of that bit of wisdom we'll tack on the Poker Pigeon's Cash Game No-Limit Postulate #2: **The amount of money needed to play in a no-limit cash game depends on** the size of the forced bets. While this statement might seem elementary to the competent players among you, the concept of "the bigger the blinds, the bigger the game" is one that newcomers seem to have a tough time getting a grasp on. The needed buy-in to play limit poker is easy to figure out because you know in advance the maximum bet structure, but many people think that no-limit poker by any name is still no-limit poker, since the amount of the blinds don't limit the amount of the wagers. But think for a minute— and then do the math. In a no-limit game with one- and two-dollar blinds, a five-hundred-dollar bankroll will take you many times around the table, and you can exercise patience until you're comfortable enough with your pocket cards to play a hand. In a game with fifty- and hundred-dollar blinds, five hundred bucks won't last until the water gets hot, and you're much more likely to piss off your buy-in with less than pristine downcards.

While I can teach you a few postulates and rules of thumb, playing no-limit poker in a cash game is pretty much of a crapshoot—and this statement is even truer when you're talking about a tournament. While experts generally agree on the best playing strategy when it comes to limit poker, these same wizards are all over the map when spouting wisdom about no-limit games. Forty years ago the game was much simpler, when everyone adhered to the Sklansky formula in picking out starting hands and, really, played no-limit the same way they played limit poker. The only difference was that bets in no-limit were generally larger. But then along came Doyle, and Brunson's philosophy completely changed the game. Correction, that's not exactly true. Brunson patterned his own play after Johnny Moss's, then introduced Moss's system, with a few wrinkles, to the rest of the world.

According to the no-limit honchos Brunson's power system is the berries, and since it's pretty hard to argue with success, let's look at a few lessons learned from watching Brunson and reading his books. He does two things that are vastly different from the way we were taught years ago. First of all, Brunson plays starting hands in no-limit poker that few players would—and I'm not talking about an occasional pigeon move where you play weak hands strictly as a come-on. Brunson plays hands regularly that most people would throw away, the difference being that Brunson knows how to play these cards as few people do. When he limps into a pot he might have aces, and when he raises before the flop he might have 10-2 in the pocket (the starting hand of 10-2 is actually nicknamed "Doyle Brunson," because the King won the World Series' final pot with that hand two years in a row). The method to this apparent madness is that while he'll lose with weak starting cards a high percentage of the time, just as anyone would, the one occasion in five when Brunson wins, the pot is going to be a monster and will more than make up for the ones that got away. Where limit poker is a game of percentages, no-limit wins and losses hinge on pot size rather than consistent skillful play. And Brunson has the luxury of seemingly limitless buy-in money. (I won't speculate on his ace in the hole; I've heard rumors, but have no proof of the backer's identity, though it's got to be someone with pockets down to his ankles.) He brings enough to the table so that he's always got the most money and can afford to gamble where most players can't.

The other glowing oddity in Brunson's game is his aggression. Aggressive play has always been the way to go in a limit game, but back in the day, most no-limit guys preferred to lay in the weeds and set traps with their monster hands. (In fact the hide-behind-the-lick-log method continues to survives in some camps even today, mostly due to aspiring Hold 'Em players having seen the movie *Rounders*. Just as the Matt Damon character did in the picture, novice players try to copy Johnny Chan's strategy against Eric Seidel in the final hand of a World Series of

Poker Main Event that happened sometime around the Civil War. Chan slow-played the nuts into Seidel—a small straight, six-high if my memory serves me right—and wound up with the World Series bracelet for doing so. Good movie, bad example of top-flight play. The hand in question is taken out of context, is a specific strategy designed by a pro to fit a certain circumstance, and is atypical of the way successful no-limit guys normally do it—and that group includes Johnny Chan. I used to play a great deal of limit poker across the table from Chan at the Golden Nugget, back in the day when he'd just blown in from Houston and sat around in a cap with "Luv Ya Blue" written on the crown in honor of Dan Pastorini, Earl Campbell, and the boys. In those days all of us so-called sharks thought that Chan was an incredibly poor player who had to get unbelievably lucky to win, which he somehow did consistently. After many painful lessons we finally figured it out; Chan won *because* of his reckless style of play, not in spite of it. He stole countless pots from the tightasses at the twenty-and-forty tables, and this driving style served him well when he graduated up to the big-boy games and became a consistent winner. Forget the slow-play scene in the movie. Aggression, thy name is Chan.)

Brunson's books advocate a go-for-broke style of play that works well for Brunson (and for Chan, and for Chip Reese, and for three or four others I can name), but keep the following in mind (and I'll say this in the form of a brand-new Pigeon's Postulate that just occurred to me as I was writing this paragraph, so feel blessed that you are a witness to genius in its embryo stage)—Poker Pigeon's No-Limit Cash Game Postulate #3: **Doyle Brunson's so-called Super System is a method of bullying a no-limit game by running over any and every player who gets in the system player's way. Basically, one can cut through the red tape and get to the meat of the Super System philosophy by simply stating that any time Brunson's opponent** weakness (generally by checking to Doyle, but also by .ing off tells that, apparently, no one else but he can re.d), Brunson puts heat on that player by shoveling piles of chips into the pot, no matter what his own pocket cards happen to be. It is an effective and intimidating style of play, especially against people unaccustomed to the sky-high stakes, and since very few have the intestinal fortitude to call Brunson down with marginal hands, he wins pot after pot basically by getting away with murder. The best way to handle the big-boy no-limit game is to stay as far away from it as possible. Some of you will ignore this advice, however, so heed this next bit of wisdom at all costs: Brunson's style of play works only because, when the sucker gets up the nerve to call him down or when the sucker happens to be checking the nuts into him, Doyle merely has to give the high sign to the house man and another pile of chips as big or bigger than the first pile will appear in front of him as if by magic. So the only way for you, as a novice, to attack these games is to have near-unlimited resources. If you can keep bringing more ammunition to the table for long enough to survive a succession of losing hands, then eventually you'll hit on a series of hands that will make you well and then some. The problem with the super system is that most people with the resources to play it have made their fortune in business, don't need any more money, and have better things to do than fuck around in a poker game where they are a serious underdog. If you're determined to play for high stakes, stick to the limit games, and if $4,000-and-$8,000 isn't sufficient, just tell the boys at the Bellagio that you'd like to play higher. They'll be more than glad to accommodate you.

End of cash game no-limit poker instruction.

(And incidentally, if you'll go back to the beginning of this chapter and read the foregoing few pages again, something will dawn on you that you may have missed during your Walter Mitty–like dream of sitting at the table along with Doyle, Howard, Daniel, Phil, and the crew. If you should miss the true meaning of this chapter a second time, I will give you a C for your effort, and then clue you in as follows: *The main reason to avoid no-limit games, if you buy into this book's philosophy, is that all of your pigeon moves will pass undetected. So you come into a pot in early position with shitty cards. So what? So does Brunson. And forget trying to raise expert eyebrows with the Weak Player's Fourth-Street Check-Raise or the old Black Widow trick, because Brunson's going to put you all-in before you can pull any of these stunts—or if you do make it to the turn without all of your chips in the center, when you pull your silly check-raise trick, Brunson's simply going to throw his cards away.*)

And with the cash games out of the way, now we're ready for the tournaments. So this is it, the alpha and omega of poker. This is the part where you learn to win the World Series of Poker as a total unknown (and you better endorse this book on TV when you do). Ready for your millions? I thought you probably were.

So let's go, already.

Just like the Harrah's CEO, when he tells you in his TV ad not to gamble when alone, depressed, or constipated, I'd be remiss if I didn't alert you to the true likelihood of pissing your ten thousand dollars away by entering the World Series Main Event. And yes, the winner gets millions, and yes, someone's going to win it and it might be you, but that's also true with the lottery and you can play the lottery for a buck. Maybe ten grand is chickenfeed to you, but I grew up in an era where it was a lot more than chickenfeed, and the thought of losing ten thousand dollars makes me cringe to this day.

So before you turn your money over to the tournament operators, consider this: *Joseph Hachem won seven million dollars for besting a field of 5,600 in the 2005 Main Event, so let's take out our microscope and look at what really happened in regard to this extraordinary payday. Hachem was one guy out of 5,600 entrants. His ten thousand dollars turned into seven million at the end, so his one in 5,600 gamble returned a payout of 700 times his entry fee, one eighth of the payout he would've gotten if his prize had equaled the proper odds against him.*

There is no worse gamble in the universe than the one Hachem took and won. The odds in the house's favor at casino blackjack, craps, roulette, or whatever are miniscule compared with taking 700 to 1 for your money when your real chances of winning are 1 in 5,600. Your chances of hitting five lottery numbers plus the Monkeyfuck Ball (or whatever they call the ultimate tie-breaker) are approximately one in 34 million, but the initial payout of four million is bit less than one-eighth of the proper odds, and there are actually times after a number of weeks without a winner when the lottery payout *exceeds* the odds against you winning. *At no time after the initial drawing are the odds against you winning the lottery worse in relation to the payout than the money Hachem received for his ten-thousand-dollar entry fee.* And yet the Big-Time Poker Guys all turn up their noses at lottery nuts and casino-game addicts for taking the mathematical worst of their gambles and claim that they stick to poker because it's strictly a game of skill.

Want more? Well, you're going to get it whether you want it or not. Even the guys who barely finished in the money in the WSOP Main Event were royally screwed; 500th place, (the last place in the tournament that won anything at all) for example, paid $12,500, or $2500 more than the entry fee, which comes out to a 25 percent profit when the actual odds of finishing in the money are *500 in 5,600, or slightly less than one in eleven.*

And yes, I saw Greg Raymer's television interview just as you probably did. The 2004 Main Event winner, who remarkably finished in 34th place one year after he won the whole enchilada, opined in an interview that he considered the odds against him winning to actually be about 1,500 to 1 because his skill level increased his chances of winning about three times. While he probably is a better player than 90 percent of the entrants, I totally disagree with his odds calculation. He was taking the figure off the top of his head, of course, so I'm not really knocking his statement, but with 5,600 folks jockeying for tournament position, I doubt that the best player in the field has better than a 5 percent edge over the worst when it comes to winning the bracelet. In other words I think the true odds against Raymer were over 5,000 to 1, though I confess that my figure comes straight off the top of my head, just like Raymer's calculation.

But let's assume for a moment that Raymer was right and that the true odds of his winning were 1 in 1,500. The payout of 700 to one is less than half of what Raymer should have received had he won, *and that's still a worse gamble than you can get in any game in any casino in the whole wide world, bar none.* You'd actually be better off taking your ten grand over to the crap table and putting it on the pass line, and trying to turn ten thousand dollars into seven million by letting it ride each time that you won (assuming that the house would let you bet that much, which they wouldn't). On the crap table you would surpass seven million dollars on your eleventh roll, and you'd receive a payoff of 700 to 1 for your money when your chances of making eleven consecutive passes are just about 1 in 900, still far-and-away better odds than the payout Raymer would have received on winning a second consecutive Main Event, even if the odds against him in the WSOP were only 1,500 to 1.

Still not convinced? Obviously you're not, because you've ducked past me on your way to the tournament's registration booth, hundred-dollar bills stuffed in your pockets, and have run through the casino in a serpentine pattern as I tried diving shoestring tackle after diving shoestring tackle trying to keep you away, all to no avail. I make one final lunge, grasping in desperation at your stack of money. You stiff-arm me and slide ten thousand dollars into the booth. I collapse, spent, to the floor. In seconds you've registered and walked away, leaving me there to deal with my sorrow alone.

Now that you're committed, you feel better. You spend the night at the Rio, in a mid-price room at a reduced rate for tournament participants (as opposed to the free VIP suite you could have had if you'd put your ten grand in the casino cage and agreed to risk your bankroll at craps or blackjack), have an early breakfast at the Rio, and try to appear cool and collected as poker pros you've seen on television eat at the next table (Christ, is that Hellmuth? Jesus, you think it is). The pros are completely at ease, and there's even some good-natured ribbing going on. You're jealous; your insides are wound up like a yo-yo. At a quarter to nine you enter a room the size of the Super Dome, peer out at three hundred poker tables in a jumbled-looking pattern, and gape in amazement when you learn that three hundred tables aren't even enough and that tournament participants will play in daily shifts until the field shrinks to one thousand. You find your name and table number on a seating chart and make your way to your assigned place to sit five minutes before the tournament is to begin. You're disappointed that there are no name players at your table, at least none that you've heard of. You shake hands with a lawyer from Chicago and a plumber from Phoenix as the dealer arrives with her chip rack, breaks open two new decks and spreads them so that all can see that fifty-two cards are in both, pops open an electronic shuffler, stacks one deck inside, and hand-shuffles the other. At straight-up nine a guy in the center of the room yells through a microphone that the tournament is under way. Across the way, so far in the distance that you can barely see, television cameras roll at the featured table.

So here you are. You've read Brunson's *Super System* and *Super System II* four times each, front to back, and you've committed the entire three-book series of *Harrington on Hold 'Em* to memory. Now it's time to show 'em that you *belong*, baby. You repeat a cardinal rule under your breath as you pick up your first hand and peek at your pocket cards.

The rule that you whisper, hereafter known as Tournament Cardinal Rule #1: **Your goal in the opening rounds of any tournament should be survival. Since everyone starts out with the same buy-in, there will be no overpowering stacks up against you early on, but as the action progresses you should pay close attention to which players at your table win the most pots and have the most chips at any given time. You don't ever want to play head-up against a player who can put you all-in and break you unless you have very strong pocket cards or happen to flop a very big hand. Against players who have fewer chips than you, you can play more marginal hands and possibly even run small bluffs since those players will be acutely aware of your own stack of chips and will therefore fear you. A good first-day rule of thumb is, you should never risk more than half of your stack on any given hand unless you have a cinch winner. All-in bluffs should be reserved for later on, when the field has shrunk to the point that the size of the pots makes bluffing worthwhile.**

Great in theory, the voice inside your head—me—says, *but what's a big hand and what's a marginal hand? And if you've got a big hand, how do you know the other guy doesn't have a bigger hand? And what do you do if a player with more chips than you bets an amount that would put you all-in and you don't have the nuts but have two pair or a set? Is your hand "really strong" enough that you should call. The spoken strategy sounds good, but it's got more holes in it than Swiss cheese.*

There's no question that good strategy matters in a freeze-out tournament, but not nearly as much as the strategists want you to believe. The eventual tournament winner will be the one holding the most cards at the right time, and making the luckiest guesses (notice I didn't say "the best reads") as to their opponents' cards. The guy who wins the bracelet will draw out several times during the length of the tournament.

And those are the main reasons that I don't believe any one player in the Main Event has more than a minute advantage over any other player, especially considering the size of the field these days. Way back when, we felt that no one but a professional could win the World Series of Poker, and we all kidded ourselves into believing that amateurs in the field were giving their money away. In fact they were, but no more so than the rest of us. Pros won the first few World Series because only pros were entered. Johnny Moss became the initial champion because the other players *voted* him in, and since Moss was considered the Grand Old Guy of poker at the time, who in hell else were they going to vote for? The following year, Moss retained his title by triumphing over a field of exactly six players. When Amarillo Slim Preston won, he beat a field of eight.

Far cries from 5,600, what?

So am I saying that no-limit poker is all luck? Of course not; in fact, I believe that pros with serious backing are big favorites in any cash game, largely due to the size of their stack of chips. But where tournaments are concerned, I consider a 5 percent edge to be a "big favorite," opposed to the general belief that the pro's advantage is much, much greater. There is one question that it's tough for me to skirt, however, and I hear it often.

The question: *If there's that much luck involved in winning a tournament, then why do you see the same guys at final tables throughout the WSOP, year after year after year?*

And that statement holds a lot of water, not only at first glance but after careful analysis. Well, it's a free country and you can believe what you choose to believe, of course. But you'll have to grant me the same privilege, and I don't believe that the same players are in contention as often as the television producers would have you think. I've got several points to back up my argument, the first few of which are on fairly solid ground, though my last point will reek of voodoo the first time you hear it. So here I go.

First point: It's very true that when you watch the WSOP on ESPN, you will see the same players over and over, just as you'll see Tiger Woods on TV whether he's leading the tournament or fighting to make the cut. So when Jesus Ferguson gets eliminated on the first day of the WSOP, he bows out along with all of the unknowns, but the intense TV coverage centered around him gives the *impression* that Ferguson has survived for much longer than he really has. Also, there is a core of about fifty professionals who have captured the public's eye, and ESPN puts as many of these folks as possible at "featured tables" in the early going. Who plays on which day in the Main Event is strictly the luck of the draw, but once the daily lineup is established, the tournament hosts can tweak the seating arrangements as they choose— and that, dear friend, is the reason that you sit with the lawyer from Chicago and the plumber from Phoenix, with the cameras so far from your table that you'd need binoculars to keep track of the featured players. As player elimination shrinks the field, the tournament runners will combine the winners from their respective tables into smaller groups, and continue to combine winners to move the tournament along towards its climax. So if there are roughly 2,400 entries playing daily at the Rio at first, and if you divide the 2,400 into four imaginary brackets of 600 players each, and if the 25 big-name professionals playing that day are all in the same bracket, then the chances are strong that a few of these pros will survive their way through the field and be around for the late action downtown at the Horseshoe. (Do you believe that Greg Raymer moved to the same table as Mike Matusow in the '05 event, so that the two could continue the verbal sniping that they began in '04, strictly by coincidence? If you do, then I got a bridge in Brooklyn and all that jazz.) I believe that if you should see nine yo-yos from Paducah at the final table a couple of years in a row, then the TV folks would arrange some sort of bye for certain players so as to practically guarantee their presence when the final action rolls around.

So now's your chance to counter with, "If you're right, and no one has a serious advantage in the World Series, then how come two guys have got ten bracelets each and another guy's got nine and another guy's got six—"

Yeah, I know, and so on and so on and so forth. In 2005 Johnny Chan claimed his tenth WSOP title as did Doyle Brunson, T.J. Cloutier got his fifth or sixth, and Phil Ivey got his fifth or sixth as well. I've got two arguments as to why certain players win repeatedly. First of all, none of these superstars claimed bracelets in the Main Event, but in tournaments with much smaller fields (Chan won a 425-person event while Brunson triumphed against 300 some-odd, and Cloutier and Ivey beat similarly numbered fields)—and even though skill matters, as the number of entrants grows the pros' chances shrink, so in smaller fields the cream rises to the top more often.

And secondly, you must keep in mind that the earlier mentioned core of around fifty well-known, Las Vegas–based, tournament-savvy pros *appear at every single WSOP and enter every single WSOP event every year,* while of the 5,600 Main Event participants in 2005, probably 5,000 entered that tournament and that tournament alone. If there are forty to forty-five events a year, and if fifty pros enter every single one, then it would be a rarity when a name player *didn't* come out on top in a few.

That's that for me being logical. Now here comes the argu-

ment that might cause you to call for the little men with the butterfly nets. As a lead-in to what I call my Kolchak Theory (Kolchak
being the guy that Darren McGavin played on TV, the one who
knew that werewolves and Bigfoots were around when everyone
else believed that he was nuts), I've got to hark back about
twenty-five years to a conversation I had with Bill Smith, several
years before he triumphed in the WSOP Main Event himself. At
the time many poker pros considered Smith one of the greatest
players alive, though he'd never won a Las Vegas tournament.
One afternoon I sat beside Bill in a cash game, and since both
of us were having one of those days where you mostly look at
'em and toss 'em in, we began to visit a whole lot more than
we normally would have. It was shortly after the World Series,
and Bill had just returned from Las Vegas empty-handed one
more time. Sometime during the afternoon I said to him, "Bill,
everybody knows you're the nuts as a poker player, so why do
you think that people like Brunson win tournaments over and
over, and players just as good never seem to?"

Smith didn't hesitate. He took off his glasses, looked me in
the eye, and said, "Luck."

To which I, a guy who'd been taught that poker was strictly
a game of skill, said, "*Huh?*"

"I know what that sounds like," Bill said, "but let me tell you
something. Last week I was in a side game at the Horseshoe,
and Doyle pulled a chair up behind me and sweated my cards.
An hour went by and I never so much as smelled a pot, and the
time came when I had to go to the bathroom. I told Doyle to
take my place, so he slid into my seat and played on my money
while I went to the can. I was gone five minutes, and when I
come back there was a stack of chips in front of Doyle that Rin-
Tin-Tin couldn't jump over. In the five minutes I was gone he'd
picked up two flushes and a full house, I swear to God. And then
I took my seat back and Doyle left, and guess what. I never won

another fuckin' pot. Most people dismiss luck as a factor overall, but I say that Doyle Brunson's the luckiest S.O.B. that ever walked."

At the time my reaction was the same as you're likely having right now, a loud sigh followed by, "Awwww." But you've already read this far in the book, so please don't slam the covers together and toss the whole thing in the trash. At least not yet. Hear me out.

This is probably the only poker instruction book you'll ever read that acknowledges luck as any sort of significant factor. Most so-called experts will never say that winning is controlled by anything other than precise, steely-eyed concentration and strategy, and will also claim that the only times that luck ever enters into the equation are the few occasions when the sucker comes out on top. There is a good reason for these pros' position; if they ever admit that they've been plug-lucky to win over the years, who's going to look up to them as experts? Hell, they think, anybody can get lucky, but in poker, skill will out in the long run.

Think. Do you believe in lucky streaks? If you answer that question honestly, of course you do, and so do people named Brunson and Hellmuth and Ivey. Everyone who's ever gambled at anything—and that includes those who are addicted and have lost everything that they could lay their hands on to the casinos—everyone has gone through periods when they simply cannot lose. I once met a man who'd been to federal prison for fraud, and who acknowledged that he committed his crime to get the money to cover his gambling losses. But this same guy had a streak once upon a time where, in a period of a couple of weeks, he won over two million dollars in Las Vegas casinos playing craps. He eventually lost it all back and then some, but for that two-week period he was king of the world. So there's an example of a two-week lucky streak, and we'll all agree that two-week lucky streaks happen, right?

So how about a lucky streak that goes on for a month? Can that happen as well?

"Of course."

A year?

"A year? Well, uh, sure—but that would be unusual."

Well, then, how about a lucky streak that continues for a lifetime? Is that one conceivable?

"*A lifetime?* Now wait a minute . . ."

No, *you* wait a minute. If winning streaks exist, and if cards have no memory, why couldn't a person's winning streak begin at birth and continue for more than seventy years? It's possible, and not only that, a large number of poker professionals believe, in Brunson's case, that's exactly what's happened to the guy.

But hold it. Before you run to Brunson and tattle on me, I'm not saying that the Guru of Poker has won for all these years only because he's dumb lucky. Do you think I'm crazy? (*Don't answer that!*) Doyle Brunson is without question one of the best poker players who ever lived. I'm only saying that when you mix such awesome skill with more than one's share of plain-old luck, the combination is just about unbeatable. To appreciate just how lucky Brunson's gotten at times, you've got to look at the cases of a few other players of equal caliber.

1. Bob Hooks. A native Texan like Brunson, Bob Hooks is a former Southwest Conference football player who, in the 1960s and '70s, had every bit as much of a reputation as Brunson, if not more so. Like Brunson, Hooks moved to Las Vegas, and Bill Boyd (an old-time World Champion 5-card stud player who managed the poker room at the Golden Nugget) made him into a card room greeter. This meant that Hooks's job was to lure in the customers, and Bill Boyd couldn't have cared less how much of their money that Hooks separated them from once they got there. Bob survived in Las Vegas for a number of years, but eventually his cards soured, and he had to return to Texas with his pockets empty. He's still around, having run poker games in Dallas and vicinity, in Mississippi for a time, and more recently in Tyler, Texas, but Hooks has never received the fame and fortune that has befallen his old buddy Doyle.

2. Chip Reese. This is a guy you've probably seen on Poker Superstars. Called the best cash game player alive by his peers (including Brunson), Chip Reese has had the worst streak of luck known to man for quite a few years now. In one made-for-television superstars event, he came up against Howard Lederer in a hand that should have been christened the Battle of the Bad Luck Twins, Lederer having never made a showing in any World Series of Poker since a fifth-place finish around twenty years ago. Reese took his two 10s up against Lederer's A10, got a miracle flop with the case 10 as the high card on the board, put his opponent all-in by playing the hand brilliantly, then watched helplessly while Lederer built a four-flush on the board to go with the lonesome ace of spades in his hand (it should be noted that that was the only time Lederer's drawn out on anyone lately, and that usually he's on the other end of the stick). Such beats have become vintage Chip Reese, though even Brunson will tell you that as far as poker skills go, Brunson himself can't hold a candle to the man.

3. Bobby Baldwin. As a kid out of Oklahoma, Baldwin won the Main Event back in the 1970s, and for a time received well-deserved recognition as the best player alive. But then his own cards went so far south that he had to give up the game, and today he holds a square job in management at the Bellagio. Bobby Baldwin hasn't been a factor in any tournament in close to twenty years, but if you'd predicted that back in the early '80s, someone would have fitted you for a straitjacket.

That's only three cases, but the pathway is strewn with the corpses of countless others who've failed to make it in spite of their talent. Brunson, on the other hand, has never wavered and never fallen from the top rung. And if you doubt that luck plays a factor in such success, go back and watch Brunson's most recent tournament win, in the five-thousand-dollar buy-in no-limit event at the 2005 WSOP. The last four hands that Brunson played were all-ins where he took the worst hand *in every single one* and drew out on the best hand. In one of those hands he took AJ up against AK and caught *two jacks* on the flop, for Christ's sake. In the final hand of the event—and this one made even Brunson blush—he went all-in with 10-3 in a stone-cold bluff, got called down by a man who held KJ, then caught a 3 on the flop and took the prize when his opponent failed to pair. As Brunson grinned at the camera and held up one finger and a thumb-and-forefinger circle to form the number 10 (his tenth bracelet, get it?), you could practically hear the groans from the other players in the background.

Some poker players are luckier than other poker players, period, and, great player that he is, Doyle Brunson has come out luckier than the rest year after year after year. Luck matters. Color me crazy, but it really does.

And now, back to you. When we left you, multiple pages ago, you'd just gotten ready to begin your first WSOP Main Event, and had just uttered a well-worn cardinal rule under your breath and peeked at your first set of pocket cards.

Guess what. The first day has come and gone and you're still in the fray. You're playing so well that you can't believe it—oh, hell, you did violate Cardinal Rule #1 and take AK up against AQ once (you know, the time you thought you had a tell, but then it turned out that the other guy just had a cold), did go all-in and almost lose your cookies when a Q,Q,J flop appeared, but then your skill won out when you caught one of three remaining 10s on the end to make a straight. You excuse *that* dumb-lucky draw-out, rationalizing that the guy should have never been in there with AQ to begin with, and thinking that it's about time that *you* drew out instead of the other way around. The point is that you're a *player*, baby, and you've lasted longer than four of the television stars that you saw stalking out of the room with their tails between their legs. As you leave the arena for the day, you see me slouched against a wall and sneer at me in triumph. I roll my eyes.

The following day is a tough one for you because that's when the second shift of the Main Event takes over the Rio card room, and leaves you out of action and wandering around town with your thumb up your nose. You do get a call from one of your friends back home, who tells you to steer clear of Dan Harrington because the guy never bluffs. You know that your friend is full of it, because you watched Harrington run a stone-cold bluff during last year's series, but you thank him for his advice and don't let on what you really think. Your friend asks you if any of the hands you played will avoid the cutting-room floor and make it onto the TV broadcast. You know good and well that not a single foot of film got shot at your table, but you tell your friend that you think your big win—where you knocked out the lawyer from Chicago—was a keeper. In the evening you order the crabmeat melt from room service, eat about half of the sandwich, then toss and turn through the night. You order porn from PPV, but you barely even notice that the set is turned on.

On the third morning of the Main Event you arrive bleary-eyed at the Rio, and take your seat among the two thousand souls who've made it this far along with you. And just as you did as a prelim to the first day's action, you repeat Cardinal Rule #2 under your breath as you wait for the dealer to arrive.

Tournament Cardinal Rule #2: **The second and third days of a tournament are moving days. This is the time when sur-**

vival takes a backseat to chip accumulation because there's no point in hanging around for the finals unless you have the chip count to do some damage. Today you will zero in on those with smaller chip stacks than yours and put them all-in and out of the tournament while steering clear of the monster stacks that can eliminate your own.

Once again, good theory, I say inside your head, *but what if one of the tournament bullies tries putting you all-in when you've got a monster hand yourself? And what if one of the people that you plan to pick on as a weakling should happen to—*

"Shut the fuck up," you tell me under your breath. The dealer spreads two new decks for all to view, then drops one into the electronic shuffler, hand-shuffles the other, and puts out the first two-card hands of the day. You pick up your pocket cards and have a peek at them. For the second day in a row you see no table-cams nearby, and the guys operating the minicams are at the far end of the room along with their lighting crews. I try to say more, but you hush me once again.

So you make it through the early hands without incident, and around mid-morning you pick up JJ in late position after a player two seats left of the blind has raised, and no one has called by the time it's your turn to act. You quickly estimate the raiser's chip count to be about half of your own. Aha! You announce "all-in" with a forward sweeping motion of your hands. The button man, small blind, and big blind muck their cards. The original raiser's fingers tremble as he peeks at his pocket cards, then checks you out for a tell. You've already snugged your Aviators up and show him none. He puts the rest of his chips in the center. You show your jacks with flair.

The other guy turns up KK, and folds his hands in front of him.

Christ, you're screwed! The flop produces junk. Fourth Street is a deuce and the third K that your opponent picks up on the river adds insult to injury. You try to keep your cool as 50 percent of your stack goes sliding to the other end of the table, but you're churning inside. The loss has reduced your chip count to the smallest at the table. There's no one left for you to bully. The road home beckons.

Yesterday you didn't lose a single pot in which you played, but now despair puts you over the edge. You're on tilt, even though you don't have the experience to recognize the feeling. There's a sinking sensation in the pit of your stomach, and you're in give-up mode. You want it all over with. You were crazy to enter this tournament to begin with, and you may as well have flushed your ten grand down the toilet. I'm still inside your head but resist the urge to fill your ears with hollow laughter. I feel a surge of pity. Sure I told you so, but I'm not the kind to gloat.

The very next deal gives you the K♠ and the 2♥ as your pocket cards. When it's your turn to act, you push the rest of your stack into the center; you no longer care about the money and just want out of this room. The other players recognize your distress, though none show the slightest bit of sympathy. The button man calls you and raises the balance of his chips so as to knock out the rest of the competition; he wants you for himself. The player in the big blind position calls. He has the most chips of the three of you, and, as Big Blind announces his call, the button man groans out loud. Big Blind never would have called in his position without one monster of a hand. The dealer isolates the side pot, the one in which you participate, off to one side. The amount that you don't have covered is up for grabs between Button Man and Big Blind. Button Man rolls over the A7 of hearts. Big Blind smirks and shows AA, a club and a spade. You turn up your K2. Somewhere on your left, one of the other players snickers. Button Man knows that he's as good as finished, and stands to put on his coat. You're soon to be out of the tournament as well, but you keep your seat. You close your eyes and utter a futile prayer.

The dealer burns, then pops the next three cards off of the deck, and exposes a flop of 2,2,2. You've just made quads, and both Button Man and Big Blind are now drawing dead. Your panic leaves you, replaced by icy dead calm; you've outplayed your opponents one more time. Big Blind murmurs, "Fuck."

The dealer completes the board to determine who gets the part of the pot that you can't win. Big Blind's aces stand up to eliminate Button Man, who's already stalked halfway to the exit before Fourth Street hits the table. Big Blind now has fewer chips than he started with even though he won the main pot. You've tripled your stack. As you carefully arrange your chips into five-thousand-dollar piles, one of the floor men comes over. A woman has complained about Big Blind's foul language when your quads appeared, and Big Blind has to pay the price of swearing with a thirty-minute penalty. As Big Blind goes off to serve his sentence, he glares at you.

What a lucky shit, I say inside your head.

Fuck you, you reply in thought, though you're careful not to say the words aloud.

Your good fortune continues throughout Day Three and on into Day Four. In the closing hand on Day Three you come into a pot with J10, catch 9,8,7 on the flop, and eliminate your sixth player of the tournament. Though you were earlier on the brink of elimination, you've battled all the way back, and the win makes you the chip leader. On your way to the exit a comely female TV assistant intercepts you, escorts you to the interview table, fixes a mike inside your shirt, powders your forehead, and arranges a giant pile of chips in front of you. Finally you're in the glare of the camera lights. Norman Chad comes over, sits across from you and launches into an interview.

At first you're tongue-tied in the presence of celebrity, but as the interview progresses, your confidence grows. You've often pictured this moment and rehearsed over and over what you were going to say, but now you forget the words that you've planned. In the end you tell Chad what a win here would mean to you, long-deserved recognition from your peers in the poker world, which sounds strangely like the same thing you've heard on television from other first-time interviewees. Finally you finish and start to leave. You're walking on air.

I'm stunned, speechless, and have exited your head hours ago, and now stand dejectedly as a shadow against the wall. As you approach me, I hang my head. You sweep past without a word.

The field shrinks to five hundred around mid-morning on Day Four. Five hundred is a significant figure because the tournament pays out prize money down through 500th place, and the survivors are assured of profit. When player number 501 leaves the room, a floor man announces the moment and a cheer erupts from the survivors. You're at your seventh table since the tournament began, and your chip count totals seven million, a commanding lead. This afternoon's play will go on until the elimination of four hundred more, with the final hundred continuing tomorrow downtown at the Horseshoe.

As if to better establish your position as the leader of the pack, you pick up AA in the pocket, slow-play the hand, and then knock out a woman who flops top pair along with a king kicker. In less than seventy-two hours you've gone from "in awe" to awe-inspiring. You've already decided that you can play with the best of them, and that you're a favorite to win in any game in the world. As you go for a glass of water during the afternoon break, even Brunson says hello to you.

The player in 101st position goes down just after five o'clock. You don't knock out 101; rather, you leave that to one of the lesser players two tables over, though you do reap the benefit along with the ninety-nine other players left besides you. The houseman stops play for the evening and tells everyone to report to the Horseshoe at nine in the morning. As you walk away from the table, rotating your shoulders and massaging the back of your neck, you glance around to see which of the name players are still left standing. Brunson's here and so is Ivey. Hellmuth left on Day One, as did Reese, Lederer, and Negreanu, and you've now outlasted them all. You *belong*, baby. You definitely belong.

As usual I'm leaning against a wall near the exit, and this time you don't ignore me. You look me straight in the eye, wink, and then pass me by while thumbing your nose.

Tournament Cardinal Rule #3: **When the field narrows down to a hundred or less and you're still alive, that's when you go into cash game mode. What's left is a tournament within a tournament. If you're still in the game, that means you've survived day one, and that you've made the most of moving time by greatly increasing your chip supply. The marathon's about over except for the sprint to the finish. Luck will pretty much rule the rest of the way, though the larger your chip stack, the more opportunity you'll have to make a few hands.**

The next morning you report to the Mecca of Poker, Binnion's Horseshoe downtown, where no one named Binnion is in charge any longer. The Horseshoe fell victim to unpaid taxes a couple of years back, and now Harrah's owns the joint. The approach is quite different than the first time Johnny Moss walked through the door after trudging down Fremont under a blazing sun. Today the lengths of Fremont Street and Las Vegas Boulevard are an enclosed mall complete with light shows on its ceiling. There's even an oxygen bar nearby. Moss would have wondered what the fuck was going on. Binnion's million in cash still sits inside a case at the entry. You pass the glassed-in money, then go on in and find your seat in the poker room.

After the gigantic open spaces inside the Rio, the poker room at the Horseshoe seems cramped in spite of the fact that there are ten tables set up with ten players at each. You think there is actually a little more seating for the gallery here, though in a room this small the size of the audience might be an illusion. You've already checked the prize list, and know that you're guaranteed to collect six figures if you never win another hand. The money pressure's off. Less than twenty-four hours from now someone's going to wear the bracelet. You have the distinct feeling that it's going to be you. You've been living your dream all week long, and your fantasy's about to become reality.

I think about whispering a warning inside your head, but I know that you'll ignore me so I remain silent. The players and dealers are all in their places. The houseman barks the signal, and the finals are underway.

With the bracelet now in sight, the players have assumed all-business attitudes. Gone are the jokes and good-natured ribbing that went on at the Main Event's outset. You feel the mood and get into it, playing the opening hands close to the vest, pitching all of your pocket cards away among the discards except for one late-position AQ. You raise before the flop with that lovely hand, but then you have to muck when the flop produces zero. During the first couple of hours, four players at your table fall by the wayside, and you get up and move along with your five companions to another half-empty table. By now you've lost track of how many tables you've played at; the number might be ten, though it could easily be more.

About an hour after you move, the cards start coming your way again. In consecutive hands you pick up AK, KK, and QQ, and win all three, delivering knockout punches to three more tournament hopefuls. You're certain that you've maintained your chip lead, though you have no clue *how much* of a lead. Your stack is more than twice the size of the next largest at your table. You knock out another contestant with your set of 3s, and a thin guy across from you catches a straight on the end to eliminate two more in one fell swoop. The houseman comes over and tells the dealer to combine with another table. This time you keep your seat as the other foursome moves from their table to yours. Now that you hold the chip lead, the TV cameras move in closer every time you play in a pot. You try to look nonchalant, though it isn't easy to do so. The attention you're receiving now could become addictive.

At the lunch break you can barely eat half of a hot pastrami in the Sombrero Room, the Horseshoe's well-known eatery. You see me lurking nearby, but now you avert your gaze and ignore me totally.

You return to action and the afternoon drags. You maintain your chip stack now by not playing any hands at all, and watch the other players duke it out. Around three o'clock a slim attractive black woman stands at a nearby table, watches while her opponent's top pair stands up against her own top pair, lower kicker, and shrugs her shoulders as she leaves the room. Her departure leaves her table half empty, so the houseman combines those survivors with you and your companions. You move to the other table, and stand behind your chosen seat as reality dawns.

There are no more tables left except for this one! You've made it to the final nine. You're acutely aware that everyone who reaches the final table wins a million, minimum. Christ, you're rich!! You can kick back and live the life.

What was once a Walter Mitty dream, now that it's a reality, wasn't a dream at all. You can remember no flaws in your play since the tourney began (or at least no *major* flaws; you may have forgotten a few hands that you won by drawing out, but that's just part of the game for a pro such as you). You've taken your place among the best in the world, and you feel that you belong there.

I hover nearby with a sinking, been-there-done-that sensation. I know what's coming, but I'm afraid to watch.

Brunson has made the final table as well. Seen close-up, his well-worn face and dancing blue eyes are mesmerizing. The King of Poker makes his presence known early on in the final table action by moving two players all-in at once, and taking the monstrous pot with his pair of tens. You mentally size up Brunson's chips, and think that with the victory, he may have wrested the chip lead from you.

As the day wears on you do your part, knocking out three more contenders. You notice Brunson watching you; while you steer clear of any head-up matches with the man, it's getting more apparent from the size of the chip stacks around the table that the final showdown will come down to you and him. You make the showdown a reality in late afternoon, eliminating the third-place finisher when your pair of deuces stands up against his AQ suited. It's now down to you and The Man. You fleetingly recall *The Cincinnati Kid,* and wonder if you look anything like McQueen.

There is a pause while the security crew hauls millions in cash from downstairs, dumps the money on the table. One guard gently places the bracelet on top of the pile of currency. The bracelet gleams in the light. Your palms are suddenly damp.

Your victory over the third place guy has made your stack slightly larger than Brunson's—it's not much of a lead, but it's a lead nonetheless. You've watched Brunson enough on television to know that he bluffs consistently. You decide to play him loose, outcome be damned.

You don't have long to wait. In the second head-up hand you pick up pocket jacks, raise two hundred thousand chips over Brunson's blind, then tremble a bit as he declares all-in. So much for playing Brunson loose; you've talked a good game to yourself, but when push comes to shove and the money's on the line it's an entirely different feeling. You muck your jacks, then feel like a fool as Brunson shows you the Q4 he's bluffed with. As he stacks his chips you're seething inside.

Brunson looks as calm as a man at the ol' fishin' hole back in Texas.

Four hands later it's your blind. Brunson peeks at his pocket cards, and moves all-in once more.

You stare at the guy, and think you spot a tick, a muscle spasm in his cheek. You think on what you've learned from my book about cold all-in moves, that they're generally bluffs, that a player with a really big hand usually slow-plays in an attempt to suck you in. You look at your own hole cards, K♠4♦. You hold the cards by the corners, and start to toss them in. You pause.

You've got Brunson beat. You *know* that you've got him beat. King high isn't that bad of a head-up hand, and Brunson has to be bluffing. He thinks you're weak and he's taking advantage. It's time to make a stand. You think your stack is still larger than his, and you can win the World Series of Poker, right here.

You announce that you call. A hush falls over the gallery. A chip count ensues and shows that you've got exactly seven hundred more in chips than Brunson. If you win this hand the tournament's over. If Brunson takes the pot, you'll be crippled beyond repair. You show your K4, and shrug. "I think I picked up a tell," you say. "Was I right?"

Brunson doesn't answer. Instead he rolls over two black aces, leans back and waits for the dealer to deal.

Your heart sinks to somewhere in the vicinity of your stomach. You try to console yourself by thinking that second-place money is still in the millions, but consoling yourself doesn't work. By God, you want that bracelet! This year it's not to be, but you're already thinking about next year. The dealer places your hand faceup alongside Brunson's, burns, and produces the flop.

You stare, openmouthed. Christ, it's K,K,4. You've made a full house already!

Brunson's expression doesn't change. He's dead to one of two remaining aces, but he's been here before and he isn't bothered. He's won a few and lost a few in his time.

Fourth street is a queen, and on Fifth Street the seven of diamonds hits the board. You've *won*, by God. You stand and shout, "Hooray!"

Brunson briefly shakes your hand, then moves away with the aid of a cane. Norman Chad shoves a mike in your face. The interview is a nightmare: you're so frightened of the limelight that your answers to Chad's questions are a jumble of words. Later you'll recall saying something to the effect that you've always known that you play as well as the Big Boys, and now you're glad that the world knows as well. Once Chad's finished with you, you tell the houseman that you'd like to keep a hundred thousand of the cash but have a check for the rest. He agrees and goes off to do your bidding. You are King of Poker for a year.

On your way out of the casino, one of the dealers hands you a folded note. It's from Brunson, congratulating you on your win and inviting you to play in his private game tomorrow. *Why not?* you think. You can now afford about anything, and you're certain that you'll be the best player in the game. You scribble your affirmative answer and return the note to the dealer. He nods and hands you another piece of paper on which he's written the time and place for the game. It's at the Bellagio, of course, at ten-thirty in the morning. And that's where you now belong.

You feel a nearby presence, and turn your head to look at me. "Don't do it," I beg. "Stick your money in your pocket and go on home."

Not on your life, you think. You're about to make a shambles of the toughest game in poker tomorrow, and why shouldn't you? You've by-God earned your spurs, and no two-bit limit player such as me is going to tell you what to do. You stiff-arm me and walk quickly away. Two security guards grab me and haul me toward the exit.

So how was the ride, Walter Mitty? I may have hammed it up a bit, but what you've just experienced is pretty much the norm for first-time tournament winners. Oddly enough, Las Vegas pros don't regard the newly victorious as any sort of threat; rather they see a sucker suddenly flush with cash, easy pickings for their daily game. And the come-ons from the vultures are just one of the pitfalls of winning a major poker tournament; there will also be offers for dot-com poker room commercials and invitations to made-for-television events such as the International Poker Superstars. You'll be asked to lecture in various cities across the country, and in every city you'll be expected to pull up a seat in the highest game in town. It's all heady stuff and all quite lethal. It will be all you can do to hang onto your money for any length of time.

In fact, the after-effects of becoming a Big-Time Poker Guy have more pitfalls than the Road to the Top, and then some. On the way up, when no one had ever heard of you, if you took a wrong turn and ended up in Brokeville, you could always take a job to build up your bankroll, then recover to the straight and narrow by playing in a series of small- to medium-limit games. But once you're a Made Man and known to all the world, circumstances change. If you could hoard your tournament winnings and return to your bread-and-butter ten-and-twenty, fifteen-and-thirty, and thirty-and-sixty games, then you could live the rest of your life in relative ease, but rare is the man who can do so. The limelight is addictive. And even after your money's gone, the *illusion* of being a Big-Time Poker Guy will linger on, and since everyone who knows anything about the game will know about your big win, you'll receive virtually limitless offers of credit for a while, until it becomes apparent to your creditors that your money's all gone and you really can't pay. When that happens, depending on who's extended you credit, you could really be in danger. I knew a man who won eight hundred thousand dollars but six months later owed over a million to various gambling facilities around the country and took his own life, ending up buried in a county grave.

As always, it's your existence and your money, and you can do as you choose to do. And since nearly all readers of this book will have no intention whatsoever of becoming poker professionals, the advice I'm giving here won't be needed very often. But on the occasions when it does come in handy, I'd be woefully remiss if I didn't lay it out for you. If you're going to play poker at a high level of skill, stay small and hidden in the shadows, and avoid games where fortunes are won or lost like the plague. Next to no one can afford those games on a regular basis, and I believe fervently that winning or losing in the big time is mainly the luck of the draw.

And with that said, it's now time for me to climb down from my soapbox and be out of here. I'm headed for a recently opened casino card room in Oklahoma, and a week from now I'll be in southern California at my favorite spot in Gardena, another Mecca of poker that's lately fallen off the radar screen. And after that, who knows? It's been nice visiting with you, and I'd like to say I hope to see you soon, but my real desire is for you to never notice if you should run into me. If I'm on my game at the time, I'll be the guy entering pots weakly from early position at times, trying to pull clumsy Fourth-Street Check-Raises, and, outwardly at least, playing poker like the biggest pigeon alive. That's my Utopia. And if I should forget myself, begin to spout poker wisdom from the side of my mouth, perform one-handed chip shuffles, and generally act like the oft-perceived version of a Big-Time

Poker Guy, then I sincerely hope you'll put on a few pigeon moves and separate me from whatever bankroll I've brought along. Believe me, if I should ever make the mistake of reverting to my ways of twenty-five years ago, then taking my money would be the biggest favor you could ever do me.